RUSH
VISIONS
THE OFFICIAL BIOGRAPHY

BY BILL BANASIEWICZ

Omnibus Press
LONDON/NEW YORK/SYDNEY/COLOGNE

© 1988 Bill Banasiewicz.
This edition © 1988 Omnibus Press
(A Division of Book Sales Limited)

Edited by Chris Charlesworth.
Book designed by Pete Hodkinson
& assisted by Sue Pownall.
Photo research by Bill Banasiewicz
and Rush.
Project co-ordinated by
Caroline Watson (London) and
Pegi Cecconi (Toronto).

ISBN 0.7119.1162.2
Order No. OP 44387

Exclusive Distributors:
Book Sales Limited
8/9 Frith Street,
London W1V 5TZ, UK.

Music Sales Corporation
225 Park Avenue South, New York,
NY10003, USA.

Music Sales Limited
120 Rothschild Avenue, Rosebery,
NSW 2018, Australia.

To the Music Trade only:
Music Sales Limited
8/9 Frith Street,
London W1V 5TZ, UK.

The vast majority of photographs that
appear in this book were contributed
by the members of Rush, their
families, friends and professional
colleagues. We are also indebted to
Dimo Safari, Deborah Samuel,
Fin Costello, Jaeger Smith Kotos,
L. Young Photo Archives (page 26),
Laura Wright, Scott Weiner (31),
Jim Bossier (23), G. Lee (78),
Bill Banasiewicz.

All lyrics reprinted courtesy of
Core Music Publishing.
All lyrics © Core Music Publishing
(Worldwide).
All rights reserved.

Readers wishing to correspond with
the author on Rush related matters
may write to : B-Man, PO Box
15924, Middle City Station,
Philadelphia, Pa 19103, USA.

Typeset by Capital Setters, London.

Printed in Scotland by Scot Print
Ltd., Musselburgh.

Geddy Lee and his wife Nancy have kept scrapbooks that chronicle Rush's career, and they allowed me to use anything I wanted, so much of the material in this book is from their personal scrapbooks.

Geddy told stories about each photo as he turned the pages through his career. I could sense a certain pride coming through him as we looked through Rush's very long, hardworked, successful life as a band.

Geddy had devoted a good portion of his own life to his music and damn well should be proud. Through the times his mother told him to be a doctor, to the times only 20 people showed up to see them, through the times that Rush were slayed by critics' pens, to executives talking of hit singles, Rush have endured. They have defied the odds and have become one of the world's most successful bands on *their own terms*.

They have legions of loyal fans worldwide who expect them to progress, change, and grow musically. This has enabled Rush to experiment with any musical style desired. They are one of the world's few bands that progress in compositions, experimentation, instrumentation, structure, and sound on every record. Each album is better than the previous one.

If each of you had the opportunity to get to know Geddy, Alex and Neil, you would be proud of them as people. They are sincere, loyal, funny, dedicated, progressive and talented with values and priorities.

Rush are taking modern music to new creative plateaux. To me, Rush truly are the world's most progressive band.

I am grateful to them all for their help in researching this book, and also to the following for their help and inspiration: my mother and father, all at SRO Productions, Ray Danniels, Pegi Cecconi, Bob Farmer, Val Azzoli, Sheila Posner, Howard Ungerleider, Charlene McNicol, William Birt, Linda Lockett, Lesley Clark, Marilyn Harris, Dave Rubin, Hugh Syme, The Rush Road Crew, Kevin Stone, Jeff Promish, Gary Bridges, Jim Sotet, Dennis Somach, Cindy Hudson, George Griffith, Ann Rubin and Walt Kostik. Also Moon, Anthem, Mercury and Polygram Records.

Bill Banasiewicz, 1988.

*i*n 1968 psychedelia ruled. Flowers and guitars, protest and imagination, dominated the airwaves and the headlines. While students around the world tried to change politics, musicians expanded the way people listened. Along with the gentler strains of The Beatles, Donovan and The Byrds, another type of music was making itself heard. Bands, mainly from England, sang about young men's blues, strange brews, and being experienced, over the sounds of bass, guitar and drums. Groups like The Jimi Hendrix Experience, The Who and Cream all shared a mixture of speed, aggression and feedback.

Thousands of kids in basements from Great Britain to the United States and Canada were occupying their time trying to emulate these new sounds.

To a 14-year-old boy who played in the basement of his house on Pleasant Avenue near Yonge and Steeles Streets in the Northern Toronto suburb of Willowdale, many of the events of the late 1960's were far away, but the feedback was as immediate as the nearest amplifier.

Alex Lifeson, the son of Yugoslavian immigrants, had been playing guitar for two years. He was given a $13 Kent Classical for Christmas in 1966 and the strings felt natural to him because he had already practised with a viola and a neighbour's guitar. The first tune that emerged from his guitar was the jingle to a Noblesse cigarette commercial.

Born in the mountain town of Fernie, British Columbia, just north of Glacier National Park, his family soon moved to Toronto, into one of its many ethnic neighbourhoods.

When his good friend John Rutsey, who lived across the street, began banging around with the drums, the two started playing together. At first John used a rented kit, but eventually his parents relented and bought him some battered second hand Slinger-lands. They shuttled back and forth between each other's basements depending on whose parents were willing to put up with the noise that week.

Other area kids soon joined in. Basement bands were formed. There was a whole bunch of kids who

Before and after – the beginnings of Rush.

would hang out together, listening to the music and carrying equipment when needed. The first band formed by Alex and John in the Spring of 1968 was called The Projection. By the end of the summer that band had broken up.

In August, Jeff Jones came in as bass player and lead singer and a formal line-up of John, Alex and Jeff was formed. They spent their evenings and weekends trying to learn the hard rock songs of the day and scheming for an opportunity to play outside their basements.

The boys were soon able to work out an agreement to play in another basement, but this time they would be paid. Their salary was $25. The gig consisted of playing on Friday nights at an oddly named coffee-house located in the basement of an Anglican Church. The Coff-In served coffee, doughnuts and music to local teens for 25 cents a head.

The band was excited, but they had a big problem. While they had been dreaming of playing, they had neglected to come up with a name for their group. So a few days before the gig they sat around in John's basement trying to come up with an appropriate monicker. They weren't having much luck when John's older brother Bill piped up, "Why don't you call the band Rush" and Rush it was.

The Coff-In was one of many so-called drop-in centres sprouting up in Canada at the time. By telling friends and acquaintances about the gig they were able to draw in nearly 30 people for the show. They were received pretty well, and with one live performance under their belts, the members of Rush were ready for a return performance. Well, at least two of them were.

The following Friday saw their new-found careers almost come to a halt. At around 5pm, just a few hours before they were due to perform, Jeff called and cancelled because he wanted to go to a party. It was time for some quick thinking, so Alex called up another bass player he had jammed with a few times.

"Often I would call Gedd up to borrow his amp. When I called him up this time, right away he thought, 'Oh, he's going to want my amp', and I said, 'Do you think you could come and play with us, because Jeff isn't coming, we don't have a bass player, and we have this gig tonight. We'll just play the songs'."

The songs consisted of half a dozen Cream tunes that most of the neighbourhood players thought they knew by heart.

Alex later told Geddy that he would have to sing. Geddy was not thrilled about this, but as the new man on board and with lead singers hard to find, he didn't have much choice. Alex had first met him in a history class at Fisherville Junior High. Their history teacher, Mr Bissle, remembers Alex as being "very likable, fun, outgoing and level-headed. I always had Alex sit right in front of me where I could reach him. Gary (Geddy) was more quiet and studious. He had his feet on the ground and was soft-spoken. The two of them would sit around the school playing their guitars all the time."

Geddy was excited if a little surprised by the request. He had never met John. "Alex used to borrow everything," says Geddy. "He borrowed my amp regularly and one day he called up to borrow me."

Gary is from a family of Polish Jews who survived the war and moved to Canada to start a new life. The name Geddy comes from his mother calling him Gary in a heavy Yiddish accent, which of course sounds like Geddy, and the name has stuck ever since.

Geddy had started out on guitar, an acoustic with palm trees painted on it. The first song he ever learned was 'For Your Love' by The Yardbirds. He switched instruments when his first band lost its bass player and the group elected him to lose two strings and fall into the rhythm section.

Geddy's début with Rush in September of 1968

was solid. When they had exhausted their repertoire of the half dozen Cream songs they knew, they played them again, and then again.

After the show the trio split the $25 and went out to eat. At the restaurant they decided Geddy was in, and Jeff was out. Their first rehearsal was set for later in the week. Jeff was already playing in another band (Lactic Acid) so his dismissal was not that big a deal at the time.

When the new version of the band assembled for practice they had a rather motley collection of equipment. Along with borrowed amplifiers and other gear, they had a few things of their own. John had his Slingerland drum kit, Alex a Conora guitar. He bought the Japanese solid body for $59. Geddy also had a Conora.

"I painted my Conora bass myself. It had all these beautiful colours on it. In those days, Cream were my heroes, and Eric Clapton had this guitar that was beautifully painted, so Alex and I thought we'd paint our guitars."

Rush rehearsed as much as possible. They slowly expanded the number of cover versions they did, and tunes by Jimi Hendrix, The Who, Jeff Beck, The Rolling Stones, Blue Cheer and Elvis joined the original set list of Cream songs. Perhaps the most unusual song in Rush's sixties repertoire was Presley's 'Jailhouse Rock' sung in Yugoslavian! The band also began writing original material. The tunes usually didn't even have names; they were mostly 12-bar blues, simple in structure, almost glued together with plenty of room for solos and hollering.

The first composition that got a name was titled 'Losing Again'. Geddy and Alex wrote most of the

music with an occasional contribution from John. The lyrics were made up on the spot.

"On 'Losing Again' Alex and I kind of hammered it out," John remembers. "I had an idea, and I didn't play a melodic instrument, so I kept repeating to Alex verbally what it should sound like. I had this song running through my head and I couldn't play it. We worked it out together and finally it sounded like it did in my head. That was our first song."

But with most of the songs, "Gedd or Alex would come in, have an idea and they'd start playing," says John. "They'd have a riff, or a chord, or a few bars of something and we'd all go 'That sounds good'. It would then be practised and we'd stop and say, 'Let's put this little bit in here'- that sort of thing. It was not unusual that somebody would have a complete concept of a song, a beginning, a middle and an end. The first song someone had totally written out was 'In The Mood'. Gedd came in and said, 'I've got a good idea for a song' and played it from beginning to end."

Rush continued playing with borrowed equipment at the Coff-In. For one show Alex managed to convince his friend Nancy Young to borrow her brother's Gibson Firebird guitar. Her brother Lindy came along for the November Coff-In show. Everyone was quite impressed as Lindy began fooling around on the piano. He met Alex, Geddy and John and eventually started hanging out with Rush and their friends.

Rush began to gig at other drop-in centres and high school dances which could pay as much as $40 for one night's work. But a lot of the band's playing was still confined to each other's basements.

Geddy's brother Allen says, "The rehearsals could have an unintentional comic note. My grandmother would be yelling about the noise and the band were playing so loud they couldn't hear her. They just kept jamming while she kept yelling and cooking."

Since volume was as important as skill, the band could be heard for blocks around. Allen would catch neighbourhood kids sitting outside the basement window and chase them away. Many of these kids would later show up at the Coff-In.

On Christmas Day 1968 Alex phoned Lindy Young and asked him to join Rush as keyboard player. He agreed and they rehearsed at Geddy's house every day during the holiday break.

"Rush was not a heavy metal band," recalls Lindy. "We were more like a blues/rock band. Geddy was singing in a low register and had not even thought of singing falsetto."

The four-piece Rush débuted the first week of January 1969 at the Coff-In. The show featured cover versions of songs by Traffic, Willie Dixon and Ten Years After. The band was beginning to evolve with Lindy's electric piano and vocals, according to John Rutsey.

"Lindy was a real good musician. In addition to keyboards, vocals and guitar, he played harmonica and drums on the side. He was a fine musician and the band evolved musically with his addition. We were really trying some different things for the time. We were getting into early Grateful Dead and things of that sort."

Throughout February 1969 Lindy began playing more guitar and singing with Rush. 'You Don't Love Me' by John Mayall which Rush covered, featured lead vocals from Lindy. The band were on a roll into March and April. They were the main band at the Coff-In and Alex was really coming into his own on guitar. The future seemed bright even at this early stage. Bright that is, until John convinced the others that Geddy's spotlight should be turned off. So in May Geddy was kicked out of the band. Alex, John and Lindy got Joe Perna to play bass and sing and the name Rush was changed to Hadrian.

Hadrian practised in Lindy's basement with a new admirer looking on, someone who would prove crucial to Rush's later success. Ray Danniels had frequently stopped by the Coff-In to hear Rush, so when he heard of a new band formed from Rush he insisted on booking them. He was 16 at the time and already an aspiring rock mogul. He even had a small booking agency named Universal Sounds. He produced shows at local high schools and drop-in centres.

"Ray was enthusiastic, talkative, a salesman type of guy," remembers John. "He asked us if we had an agent and we said, 'Of course not.' So we went in with him and he started to get us a few jobs here and there."

Ray soon became Hadrian's manager. "They were a part-time band playing in basements," he recalls. "But even then they were writing original tunes. That was the thing that separated them from the rest of the bands at the time."

In June Geddy founded a rhythm 'n' blues band called Ogilvie. He was actually having more success with his band than Hadrian. Gedd will never forget going to a Hadrian gig to help Lindy out with the words, since he now had to sing lead on most of the songs. He went to the Willowdale church instead of going to see the last Toronto performance of The Jimi Hendrix Experience.

During July Ogilvie changed their name to Judd. Ray Danniels was also booking shows for Judd, but unlike Hadrian, Judd were getting lots of work. In that same month Lindy quit Hadrian and joined Judd. Hadrian's last gig was at the Willowdale United Church. Joe Perna didn't play all that well, so when Lindy left they disbanded.

Geddy and his band Judd continued working hard right through the summer, while Alex and John were in limbo. They didn't know what to do. Finally in September Judd broke up. John phoned Gedd and asked him to reform Rush. Gedd agreed. Lindy was beginning studies at Seneca College so he didn't rejoin. He was also tired of performing; while he liked playing at parties, he was not as serious as the others, and they were now very serious.

During the autumn of 1969 while hanging out at Al Denokowski's house everyone was blown away by the first Led Zeppelin album, especially Alex, Geddy and John. They were amazed at the sound Jimmy Page achieved on a recording. Zeppelin, the proto-type heavy metal band, built on the hard rock sounds of The Yardbirds, The Jeff Beck Group and Cream, but they managed to make their music thicker, harsher and louder than anybody else. The style entranced Rush and they soon began trying to emulate Page's unique style.

By November 1969 Rush were playing heavy rock, Alex with a stack of G.B.X. amplifiers, Geddy with a double stack of Sunn amps. He was also starting to sing like Robert Plant, developing a piercing falsetto.

Lindy Young jammed with Rush in their basements once again, but this time they were playing so loud he couldn't hear his electric piano. "If you want to be in this band," said Alex, "I think you're gonna need a bigger amp." Rush were obsessed with heavy music and even their original songs took on more of a Zeppelin-like tone. Ray Danniels began dreaming of Rush as the next Led Zeppelin.

Alex, John and Geddy resumed gigging at the Coff-In where their playing improved and more people began to take notice. Orme Riches, who ran the Coff-In at the time, later told Toronto's *City* magazine about the way the band built up its audience. "At first there was just 40 or 50 kids, but as word on Rush spread attendances soared up to 300 in a space that could comfortably hold half that number. Kids from all over the city came to see Rush swamping out the locals."

This success backfired because the ever-increasing number of people coming to the shows eventually caused the Coff-In to close. Church officials thought things were getting out of hand.

Ray worked hard at getting other shows for Rush,

Rush with Mitch Bossi.

but it was difficult to find work for a power trio that did so many original songs. Sometimes at high school dances they found that their brand of hard rock did not go over well with teenagers eager to dance to the latest Creedence Clearwater Revival single. Kids would shout out "Play some rock 'n' roll." John remembers screaming into the microphone, "We're not playing fucking jazz!" One song in particular, a Rush original called 'Child Reborn', almost always drew a hostile reaction for its complex tempo changes. The band even threw a bit of 'Hava Nagila' into the number.

"You can imagine how this sort of thing went over in front of high school kids wanting to hear Top 40 tunes. It got rough at times," says John.

So the band took on odd jobs to support themselves. Alex pumped gas and worked with his father as a plumber's mate, while Geddy worked in his mother's variety store and as a part-time painter. Alex and Geddy were also still going to school. John had dropped out. All three were under pressure from their parents who were beginning to suspect that their sons might actually be planning to make music a career, not just a hobby, which was something they could not accept.

Ray's efforts at getting them gigs began to get more successful, but occasionally these shows would

be some distance from home. "They'd get out of school at three o'clock," says Ray, "and drive like hell to get where they were going. They would play high schools in Sudbury, North Bay, Cochrane, Kirkland Lake, London, Deep River and Windsor, Ontario. These cities and towns are anywhere from 200 to 500 miles from Toronto, so it was a pretty hectic schedule for kids who were going to school."

But for the guys in the band it was anything but a chore. Alex couldn't wait for the school bell to ring on the days when they were going to play. "I remember it being great!" says Alex. "We'd finish school and everyone would make their way to where the band was leaving. Doc Cooper lived across the street and most of the time he would drive us to gigs in these old beat-up limousines. We also had another guy, Larry Bach, who drove his car, and we'd put a U-haul trailer on the back with all the gear in it. We played all over Ontario and we loved it."

Rush usually played by themselves at these shows. The performances consisted of two one-hour sets or three 45-minute sets. The band played original compositions such as 'Number 1', 'Keep In Line', 'Run Willie Run', 'Mike's Idea' and 'Tale'. Also thrown in were the ever-present Cream, Hendrix, Who and Zeppelin covers as well as other hard rock hits.

As many as 200 or as few as a couple of dozen people would come to the shows. John was the band's front man, although he didn't sing. He would introduce songs and talk in between them. The stages were usually set up in high school gyms.

"There were some gigs we played in Northern Ontario where kids were lined up against the wall," says Alex. "At other times only 35 or 40 people would come to a dance, pretty dismal! Around Toronto we did pretty well, selling out to 150 or 200 people. Up north it took a couple of years before the band really got going."

Throughout 1970 Rush continued gigging and working on original material. They composed 'Sing Guitar', 'Morning Star', 'Margerite', 'Feel So Good', 'Love Light' and 'Garden Road' during this first year of the new decade.

In February 1971, the group again gained a fourth member. Mitch Bossi joined as second guitarist. Bossi, later told *City* magazine that he was a mediocre musician who was more interested in having fun and wearing flashy clothes than in making music. He only stayed with the band a few months. He told the magazine that he quit because the others took it all so seriously. He added, "I didn't see too much future in the band. They were a different kind of people to me.

They didn't worry about security, they thought everything would turn out all right." They were right.

During the late spring the band was helped by a new provincial law. The Province of Ontario lowered the legal drinking age from 21 to 18. This opened up a whole new range of possibilities for Rush. They could now legally perform in bars, although it wasn't easy to find a place that would hire them.

"I remember the first bar gig," says John. "It was really something else. We were suburban kids. None of us had really gone out drinking in bars. Ray got us a job at the Gasworks. I was petrified because this was playing for grown-up people. Everybody in those days had really lame equipment when you come to think of it. Terrible stuff. Cornball lighting, Christmas tree lights like you use in your front yard. Ian Grandy and the other roadies would painstakingly put it together. That guy did a lot of work for the band. He also helped us out at that first gig. We played really low because we thought the audience would throw beer bottles at us. We got a kind of muted reaction during the first set. Ian came up to us and said, 'Turn it up'. I was really shocked. So the second set we took his advice and went over pretty well."

The band's insistence on playing original songs caused problems for Ray. During the summer of 1971 he was able to find them only three gigs. They later called those months 'The Dead Summer'. It was during this time that Mitch was thrown out of the band. It was particularly tough for Alex who had left school and was living away from home with his girlfriend Charlene.

Ray kept on trying to convince Rush to play more cover versions. His booking business was expanding through the success of his other acts, and for a long time Rush were the most unpopular band on his roster. He'd get club owners to take Rush as a favour for having given them a more popular act.

Ray's biggest success at the time was one of the first rock bands to cover just one group's material, Liverpool, who specialised in Beatles' songs. Ray managed to set up contacts throughout Canada and in parts of the United States because of their success and was later contacted about using the group for the original production of *Beatlemania*, but the band members refused to wear costumes and cut their hair to look like The Beatles.

Rush used their spare time to develop their music and identity as a band. They continued practising and writing new material. It was about this time that they wrote 'Working Man'. Perhaps the song reflected the jobs the guys had to take to keep going. The sound of the group still echoed Led Zeppelin, but the distinctive interplay between Alex's guitar and Geddy's bass, still a band trademark, now began to emerge. One song, 'Slaughterhouse',even had a slight political tone. "It was a hard rocker," says John, "about what was happening to the environment and the animal world. Whale and seal hunts and that sort of thing."

Things picked up in the autumn and by the end of 1971 the band were regulars at the Abbey Road pub, a bar located on Queen Street in downtown Toronto. They could pull in as much as $1000 a week for six evenings of five-sets-a-night gigs. Most of the income went straight into new equipment.

As 1972 got under way they found themselves getting work in a whole series of southern Ontario bars, places like Larry's Hideaway, The Piccadilly Tube and The Colonial. They were performing many songs that later made it on to the first album, including 'Working Man' and 'In The Mood' (still an encore song).

A two-man road crew carted the equipment around in that staple of aspiring rock bands, an Econoline Van. They had amassed a fair amount of gear. Geddy was playing a Fender bass with two Sunn twin 15-inch cabinets, Alex used two Marshall four-by-twelve cabinets, with a 50-watt head and a makeshift pedal board incorporating a phaser, echo-plex and crybaby wah-wah. John would bash away on his blue Gretsch drum kit: two bass drums, two tom toms, two floor toms and a snare.

Ian Grandy, the main crew member for Rush, mixed sound and set up the drums and lights for the band. He saw them start to build a loyal following of older fans and later recalled that some even started to request individual songs like 'Fancy Dancer' and 'Garden Road', both bar-room favourites never released on record. As their club gigs gave them more money Alex expanded his musical horizons by studying classical guitar for about six months with his friend Eliot Goldner. The lessons were cut short when Eliot cracked up his motorcycle and landed in hospital.

During the early 70's rock music began to fragment. Trends that had somehow seemed to be part of post-Beatles rock began to be separated into soft rock, exemplified by singer/songwriters Carole King and James Taylor and harder types of music - heavy metal - as played by Led Zeppelin, Deep Purple and Black Sabbath.

Other bands took a more experimental route, incorporating elements of free jazz, classical and folk music into something that was called art rock. Pink Floyd, Emerson, Lake & Palmer, Yes, Genesis, King Crimson and Gentle Giant all mined this musical

terrain. While heavy metal was still the main source of inspiration for Rush, Alex's classical guitar lessons and Geddy's interest in some of the pioneering art rock bands, signalled the direction the group would take in the future.

Alex, Geddy and John often made amateur recordings in each other's basements and at various shows, and in 1972 they were able to record in a primitive studio at Rochdale College. According to Alex it was, "More like a place to buy drugs than a school."

Bill Bryant produced in the tiny two-track garage facility called Sound Horn. "It sort of made you feel like it was the real thing," says John, "even though it was a small rinky-dink studio ... it was a good feeling that we were getting to the point where we could actually put something down."

Unfortunately the tapes were later lost.

by the time 1973 rolled around Rush had five years' experience of playing in bars, high schools and drop-in centres, and managed to win over audiences in each of these performing situations. Ray and his newly acquired partner, Vic Wilson, knew that for the band to continue gaining momentum they would have to record professionally.

However, they were not having much success interesting record companies, and studio time and producers cost money, a commodity neither Rush nor their management had a great deal of. Ray and Vic knew that the only way the band could afford to record would be with an unknown producer in a small studio, overnight when studio time was cheap. Ray thought if he could get the Rush sound down on tape he would have a good chance of landing a contract with a major Canadian label.

Their first professional recording was done at Eastern Sound Studios in Toronto with David Stock producing. The plan was to come up with a strong single. Taking the advice of record company A&R men, they recorded their first, and to this day only, cover version, a hard rock rendition of the old Buddy Holly classic 'Not Fade Away'. The B-side was a Lee/ Rutsey composition entitled 'You Can't Fight It'. 'Not Fade Away' didn't have the edge of many other Rush songs of the period, although it does feature an amusing chipmunk-on-speed vocal performance from Geddy. The B-side showed more of the band as it sounded at the time and through the first album.

Once the single was completed, Ray took it around to just about every record company in Canada. But nobody would listen to it. In the early 70's few Canadian artists got record deals and those that did generally had a softer sound. Labels were looking for artists like Gordon Lightfoot, Joni Mitchell, Neil Young and Anne Murray. A heavy metal trio was about the farthest thing from these artists that could be imagined. The best offer Ray received was from London Records who told him they wouldn't sign the band but that if he formed his own label they would distribute the single. So for the

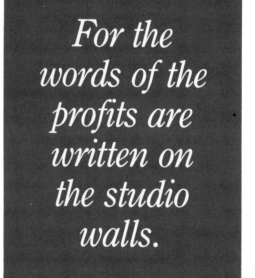

For the words of the profits are written on the studio walls.

cost of $400 and getting a record company logo made up and registering the company, Rush became a band with a single to their credit.

The disc, featuring a Moon Records label, sold a few copies in Toronto, but received no airplay. Ray and Vic thought the single would pave the way for a major record deal. They were wrong.

To make matters worse, during the summer of that year John was forced to leave the band through illness. He was also starting to question whether a career in rock music was right for him. Alex and Geddy continued playing with a pick-up drummer, but when John began feeling better they asked him to rejoin. He agreed.

With the single bombing and no record company willing to bankroll any recordings, the band hit a roadblock. Rush were doing well in the clubs around Ontario, yet they were strictly local heroes. Ray and Vic decided they would have to take a big risk. They would put up the cash to record an album and then go out and try to sell it. If the worst came to the worst they would then press it themselves and see if London Records would distribute it as they had done with the single. With the prospect of recording an entire album in front of them, Alex, Geddy and John began to think of ways to improve the songs. John thought that the lyrics particularly were lacking.

"I was going through a real struggle at this time with the band," recalls John. "I said to myself, 'I feel like quitting.' I was just a mixed-up kid and I began writing all sorts of additional lyrics for the songs, because most of the lyrics we had at the time were just whatever rhymed, whatever fitted in, 'cause we never really spent much time at all on the lyrics. So then finally we said, 'We've got to get some decent lyrics. This is silly, just saying whatever pops into your head and then trying to remember it the next night.' So we made a conscious effort and I started writing some lyrics.

"I was really having a hard time with myself and what I wanted to do with the band. I was very mixed up, I'd written a lot of lyrics and then I tore them up and never presented them. So when we went in and did the album all the old lyrics were sung. It's funny,

because to this day I still can't remember why I did that. All I can attribute that to was that, at the time, I was just very confused about what I wanted to do. I really regret it because it was an incredibly selfish, stupid thing to do. But when you are young, unfortunately you do things like that. My mood would change from day to day, I had spent a lot of time on them and some of them were decent. Anyway, that's what happened."

Meanwhile, Ray and Vic calculated that the only way Rush could afford to record would be for the band to use the cheapest studio time available, down time, in the middle of the night. So the album would be laid down late in the evening after the group finished playing club dates, shows of up to five sets which could stretch out to one or two in the morning. The band knew that they had no other choice.

Liam Birt, who helped move the band's equipment and would later become Rush's stage manager, witnessed the sessions.

"Most of it was playing in a bar from nine at night until one in the morning, packing up the gear into a van, driving it to the studio where we'd work until the wee hours of the morning. Then pack it up again, go home, get a few hours' sleep, and just keep repeating the process. It was a crazy schedule."

Geddy remembered it as a really hectic period, but since everyone was so excited about being in the studio, they were able to summon up the enthusiasm to continue. On occasions they would go in because they just had enough time to record a guitar part or a vocal. Since John never delivered the lyrics, Geddy had to sit down and write the words he had been making up off the top of his head. When the record was finished everyone gathered round to listen. They were not happy with the results.

"David Stock did a lot of commercial work, a lot of jingles and he really took the edge off the music. We realised we had to get somebody to punch it up," says John.

So Ray and Vic rounded up more money and called Terry Brown. Brown, or Broon, as he is known to his friends and co-workers, owned a competing recording facility, Toronto Sound. An English expatriate, he had worked on recordings by Bill Cosby, Procol Harum, Thundermug and Everyday People, but had never even heard of Rush until Ray called him up.

Ray, hardly a greybeard himself, explained that he had some kids in the studio who needed help. A meeting was arranged. When Terry got together with the band they hit it off right away and arrangements were made to work on the tapes the following week. Money was so tight that only two days were

scheduled to straighten out the album. Two songs were re-recorded, 'Here Again' and 'Need Some Love'. 'Finding My Way' was added in place of the band's failed bid at a commercial single, 'Not Fade Away'. Four other tunes were remixed. The total cost for the sessions was $9000.

The band were impressed with the results of the two extra days of hard work. Ray, with new tapes in hand, began knocking on record company doors once again, this time confident that a company would sign a band with an album already recorded. There was also the added factor of Bachman Turner Overdrive's popularity in the United States and Canada, but despite the success of this Canadian hard rock band, Ray found record companies were not interested in signing another. So Ray was forced to approach London Records about distributing another Moon Records release. This time though, it would not be a single, but an album to be titled simply 'Rush'.

The record kicks off with 'Finding My Way'. A prime example of early seventies hard rock, with prototype Rush guitar and bass attack, it features another highlight in Geddy's screeching, 'Sang some sad songs.'

Next come 'Needs Some Love' and 'Take A Friend'. Neither ages well, but whatever the limitations, 'Here Again' which closes the first side, shows the band trying to stretch out a bit. A slower tempo, and an effort to bring the dynamics of the song up, down, and then up again, works. It is a sign of things to come.

Side two opens with 'What You're Doing', a strong all-out rocker. The lyrics sound as if they were written in 15 minutes, but that's part of the fun. It's followed by what became the trio's second Canadian single, 'In The Mood'. When performed as part of the band's encore, it still gets the crowd to its feet. The great hook was a little too rough to become a hit, but with a line like 'Hey baby it's a quarter to eight and I feel I'm in the mood,' how could you go wrong?

1st tour T-shirt.

'Before And After' is the key song on the album to understanding where Rush would go next. What sounds like an acoustic guitar dominates a long instrumental introduction, before Geddy and Alex have some fine moments playing together.. That and the extended introduction show a different side of the band, even if the song is a great Led Zeppelin rip-off.

Finally, the album explores territory to which Rush never really returned, with the only song the band ever recorded which deals with blue collar workers, a subject which dominates the work of Bruce Springsteen and Bob Seger. When Rush returned to contemporary characters many years later, they wrote about the suburban kids they once were. But no matter what you do for a living, 'Working Man' is a great song to play loud after a bad day at work. It was always popular with audiences and stayed in the live set for many years.

The first album stacks up pretty well for a début. There are only two duds on the record and even these songs had some merit at the time they were put on tape. The disc still works because it is obvious that it was exciting for Alex, Geddy and John to be making a long-playing record. It has the raw, youthful energy of most good first albums, there are some great guitar solos, and Geddy sings with piercing youthful passion. Control would come but at that time it was good enough to kick out the jams.

Some of their earliest fans still swear by the record and say Rush were never able to muster up the same amount of energy again. But it does have major faults: no developed signature sound, Geddy

sounds like Robert Plant, and Alex plays like Jimmy Page. The pair would have to sound like themselves if they were to have a long and successful career.

London Records agreed to distribute the album, and Ray and Vic decided to take another risk. Instead of pressing the minimum amount of copies (1,000) they shelled out money for 3,500 discs, a demonstration of faith that the band would remember for years. With their limited means, the pair were betting on Rush in a major way, but the shoestring budget still showed. There was almost nothing left over to pay for the design of the album cover, so the Rush logo was placed on top of what looked like an explosion. In Canada, the colour of the logo was red.

Before the album hit the stores, the band went on a short jaunt that could be called 'Rush Times Three'. The Ontario area performances featured a triple bill of Rush , Mahogany Rush and Bullrush.

Ray and Vic also booked a co-headlining show featuring the band and the proto-punk/glam rock New York Dolls. Rush went over well with a wasted audience at the October 27 gigs at Toronto's Victory Burlesque Theatre. They literally blew the Dolls off the stage. It was a major confidence builder. For the first time they realised they could hold their own, and then some, playing side-by-side with a name act. The hall held 1,200 people for each show and it was a bittersweet victory for Geddy who felt that playing such a large hall was nerve-racking. He would have to get used to it.

The album was supposed to be released in December, two months after the Victory gig but OPEC intervened. When the oil cartel created the first energy crisis, it also had a side effect on the recording industry since vinyl is a petroleum by-product. The shortage of oil meant a shortage of vinyl, which in turn meant a delay in the album release date. Eventually it came out in January 1974.

Local radio began to pick up on the record. One local DJ said he decided to play it because he was always seeing ads in the newspaper for Rush shows at local bars. To the band it was something else. Geddy said he will never forget hearing himself on the radio for the first time. "It really freaked me out when DJ David Marsden played 'Finding My Way' on CHUM-FM."

Marsden got an unusual phone call that day. "My request lines were ringing and I believe in talking to the people, so I picked up the phone with Rush playing and the voice said, 'David, how are you doing? It's Alex calling.' My reply, 'Okay Alex, what do you want to hear?' and Alex said, 'No, I just wanted to thank you for playing our record. It's the very first

An early shot of Rush Mark I performing in Cabbage Town, Toronto.

time I've heard it on the radio.' "

CHUM-FM continued to play the disc. It also got air time in Montreal, but that was about it for radio. Still, to Alex, Geddy and John, just having a record released was a thrill.

"At the time we were one of the few Toronto bands to have an album out," says Geddy. "It was a big step for us. We moved up the ladder a few notches. Our shows began to contain almost all original material. We played bigger halls and clubs, and sales were respectable in Toronto. It (the album) still has some sort of appeal in a raw sense."

Bolstered by the release of the album and the results of the gig with The New York Dolls, Ray and Vic began going after bigger shows. But it wasn't until a month after the Canadian release of 'Rush' that the group's future would open wide.

The road to success for Canadian bands in the early seventies was either to build up a loyal audience in the Great White North, and thereby attract attention in the States, or to move to the US and be marketed as an American act. Ray had other ideas.

"Canadian managers would send their acts 1,400 miles to Winnipeg," says Ray "not even considering that New York City was only 500 miles away. My

theory was the reverse, why go 1,400 miles to Winnipeg when you could play in Cleveland or Detroit which were just a few hours drive from Toronto."

The first gig Ray was able to get in the States for the band was a non-event pop festival in East Lansing, Michigan during the early spring. This outdoor festival was not Woodstock. Only 1,300 people showed up on a rainy day at the concert site . . . a drive-in movie theatre. The audience was not familiar with the band's material and they received an indifferent reception.

With their first battle for recognition in the States a draw at best, Danniels was eager for another engagement. A favour from a friend and a pair of receptive ears would give him a triumph.

Donna Halper was Programme Director at WMMS in Cleveland, Ohio. She often listened to Canadian music and was always looking for a new sound to give her station the edge in the rating wars.

"Bob Roper, who was an A&M of Canada representative sent me this record by a group that I had never heard of. It wasn't an A&M record, so this aroused my curiosity. I picked it up, and it had a really ugly cover, and without knowing a thing about the band, I dropped the needle down on the longest cut

('Working Man') and I knew immediately that it was a Cleveland record."

Cleveland, a working class city has always been a stronghold for hard rock bands. Halper told one of her DJs to play the song that night on his show to see how it went over.

Denny Sanders found that 'Working Man' stirred quite a reaction from the blue collar audience. Many of the callers thought the song was from a new Led Zeppelin album. "They were asking about where they could get the record, and of course they couldn't - there was only one copy," Halper says. Halper phoned Ray and Vic the next day. They worked out an arrangement to have a box of Rush records sent south to Cleveland. The albums were placed in a local 'Record Revolution' store. The box sold out in a few days and it became a big deal to own a copy of the album. Ray and Vic immediately went to Jem record importers to keep the Cleveland area supplied with Rush albums. The first few shipments sold out. But this wasn't enough for the pair: Rush were selling in the United States, and they wanted another show.

"It was very important for me to get the band there," said Ray. "I felt they could do well live. So I pulled a few strings and got a date opening for ZZ Top at a 3,000 seat theatre."

The show was scheduled for June 28. Also on the bill was an obscure Hungarian band, Locomotive G-T. Halper was there to greet Rush.

"They were all nervous when they came down," she says. "They had been playing in small places and all of a sudden they were about to play to a few thousand people. For the show I stood at the back of the hall, and Vic Wilson came up and said, 'Believe me Donna, we won't let you down.' And they didn't. They put on a really good show. Even then they had the beginnings of real professionalism. It was obvious to see. It was also nice to see people in the audience knew their songs. I can't lie and say everyone was immediately won over by Rush, they weren't, but even then there was an actual hard core. Fans would shout out song titles."

Alex remembered the band getting an even better reception than Halper did. If his memory is a little rosy, it's understandable.

"I remember flying down and being all excited about it. The show went off great. We'd been getting a lot of airplay down there and we were extremely nervous. We heard we were doing well, but we had absolutely nothing to gauge it against. We opened with 'Finding My Way' and the crowd went crazy! They obviously knew the material. We got an encore, and before we could go back up for a second encore,

somebody ordered the lights turned up."

The radio airplay and word of mouth about the Cleveland show began to stir interest among US record companies. Rush were close to signing a deal with Casablanca Records. By this time the début album had sold about 5,000 copies. 3000 were bought in Canada, the rest were sold in the States.

US booking agency American Talent International began talking to Ray and Vic about scheduling live shows. The pair also got Ira Blacker of A.T.I. to help them negotiate a record deal. After Blacker left A.T.I. he became Rush's American co-manager, a relationship that ended in a dispute eventually settled out of court, which cost Rush $250,000.

Cliff Burnstein worked in the national album promotion department at Mercury Records. "It was a Tuesday morning just like any other," says Cliff. "When Robin McBride's (head of A&R and responsible for signing acts) secretary came into my office and said, 'I've got this record for you to listen to by a Canadian band called . . . Rush.' I said, 'You mean Mahogany Rush, don't you?' she said, 'No, just Rush. Robin said it was important that you listen to it'."

Accompanying the album was a letter from Ira Blacker. Burnstein put on the record and began listening. "I was immediately blown away with 'Finding My Way'. The letter from Blacker stated that WMMS in Cleveland was playing the album. So I called up Donna Halper, having heard side one. Donna said, 'We are playing the record and it's getting a great response 'Working Man' is the song.' I told her I hadn't heard it yet . . . she said, 'Wait until you hear it.' I hung up the phone, put it on and sure enough it was a motherfucker."

Burnstein knew the band should be signed. With word spreading about the trio, he did not want Mercury to lose Rush. So that very day the deal went down. Burnstein, Mercury President Irwin Steinberg and Blacker negotiated their terms via a telephone conference call. The advance was $50,000 plus $25,000 towards future recording costs.

A.T.I. and Mercury then arranged for a five-month tour that would begin on August 14. The record was set to be rush-released so it would hit the stores exactly two weeks before the tour, a mere three weeks from the signing date of the contract. There was just a few cosmetic differences from the original Moon Records' release. Basically, the label name, several acknowledgements and the colour of the band's logo on the front cover were changed. The Moon cover was red but it must have hurt someone at Mercury's head, and was changed to pink. An ugly cover gets uglier.

*W*ith an album out and a tour booked, it might be said that the band had hit the big time. However, they now had months of touring, mainly as the second or third billed act in front of them. This was something John did not want to do. He was unhappy being in a rock band, and there were also arguments about what kind of music they would play. John announced he was leaving Rush again. This time the split would be permanent. With his diabetes a strong argument against touring, the musical and personal differences closed the case.

"I was into a sound very much like that of Bad Company," says John. "At the time, Alex and Geddy envisioned the band going into other areas. I also just wasn't enjoying it any more, and that's just the first telltale sign. I wasn't looking forward to it. I could tell I was straining the friendship with the other guys. It's just a hard thing to explain. I've never been able to pin it down accurately myself. I would sort of drift off and spend more time just talking with the roadies. I knew I had to do something. If you can't go out there and enjoy yourself, you know it's time to get out."

Alex talked about the musical differences and some of the personal problems involved. "He was into the basic rock thing, and Gedd and I wanted to get a little more progressive. Our relationship was also not the same as it had been. He and I were friends since the age of eight, playing street hockey, but at this point the musical differences were happening and we didn't hang out as much as we used to, outside of working. Whereas Geddy and I would hang out together all the time. So it really was a combination of his illness, our musical differences combined with the way we were growing as three people together."

With their début US tour little more than two weeks away, the band began looking for a new drummer. A mutual friend set up an audition with the drummer of a St. Catharines area band called Hush whose name was Neil Peart. His group played the Southern Ontario bar circuit, where Neil's wild style of playing came in handy when he took on the

task of playing Keith Moon licks on his Rogers kit. Most of 'Quadrophenia' was covered by Hush. Neil started out playing piano but his interest in pounding out 'Chopsticks' soon took on a more literal form. When he was 18 he went on a musical odyssey that took him far from home.

He later told *Modern Drummer* magazine: "I went to England with musical motivations and goals. But when you go out into the big world, as any adult knows, you're in for a lot of disillusionment. So while I was there I did a lot of other things (besides playing music) to get bread in my mouth."

He ended up working on Carnaby Street hawking trinkets to tourists at a store called Gear. He also told *Modern Drummer*: "When I came back from there, I was disillusioned basically about the music 'business'. I decided I would be a semi-pro musician for my own entertainment, would play music that I liked to play, and wouldn't count on it to make my living. I did other jobs and worked at other things, so I wouldn't have to compromise what I have to do as a drummer."

He had one consolation while he was in England. He found a copy of Ayn Rand's book *The Fountainhead* on the London tube. He found Rand's tales of fiercely individualistic characters struggling to maintain their integrity inspiring. It must have seemed at the time that he had his shot at the big time and failed. He would get a second chance.

Before they heard Neil, Alex and Geddy had already listened to several other drummers. None of them had really impressed. Neil cut a strange figure coming in an old car with his drums packed into garbage cans.

"Neil came down the second day of auditions," says Alex, "and he looked really weird. He had really short hair with shorts on. He was working in a parts department, selling tractor parts. So this weird looking guy comes down with this small kit of Rogers drums, and he played them like a maniac! He was really an intense drummer! I had reservations, however, I wasn't really sure. Neil was the second or third guy we tried, so who knows. Maybe there's going to be three or four others as good. It was a bit

> *When I leave I don't know what I'm hoping to find.*

Geddy with Manfred Mann.

weird. We sat down and talked a lot. Geddy and Neil talked mostly. I had these reservations. I wasn't sure."

While Alex stood on the sidelines, Geddy was immediately won over. "After I heard Neil play, there was no one else who could come after the guy. I was convinced that he was the drummer for the band."

Neil was convinced that the audition was a disaster. "It was funny because Geddy and I hit it off right away. Conversationally we had a lot in common in terms of books and music… so many bands that we both liked. Alex, for some reason, was in a bad mood that day. So we didn't have much to say to each other. Playing together, we did what eventually became 'Anthem'. We jammed around with some of these rhythmic ideas. I thought 'Oh this is awful'."

After Neil left, Geddy tried to convince Alex that the strange looking guy was the man for the job. The argument was settled when the next drummer came in and politely played to charts he had written for all of the songs on the first Rush album.

Neil officially joined Rush on Geddy's 21st birthday, July 29, 1974. On the 30th they went out to buy equipment for the tour. "We got this big advance from the record company," says Neil. "We went down to the music store with all of us sitting in the front of the truck with Ian. Just going wild! We ran into Long and McQuade Music at 459 Bloor Street and Geddy got his first Rickenbacker (the black one). I went downstairs and picked out my Silver Slingerlands. Alex got new Marshall Amps and a Gibson Les Paul Deluxe. It was a Babes In Toyland kind of day, total fantasy. All the way home we were screaming and yelling up the highway. It was fantastic…"

With all the new equipment, the band went to work. They had less than two weeks before they had to start off for their first date. The one advantage they had was that since they were the opening act, the set would be short, 26 minutes to be exact.

Their first full US tour began on August 14 in Pittsburgh, Pennsylvania, warming up the stage for Uriah Heep and Manfred Mann before 11,642 people at the Civic Arena. The fear factor was very high. Neil's first performance with the band thus took place in front of more than 10,000 people. After seeing the crowd enter the hall Geddy had a ceremonial shot of Southern Comfort because he believed that's what 'Rock Stars' did to warm up. He was wrong.

Neil: "It was both testy and fabulous at the same time. It was the big time, and a very big gig at that."

The brief set included 'Finding My Way', 'Working Man', and 'In The Mood'. The Professor - as Neil was christened - also did a short solo, a major element

of the band's live show to this day.

This concert of firsts also introduced road manager Howard Ungerleider to the scene. Howard worked for A.T.I. and he was along to shepherd the lads through their first major tour. Also accompanying the band were Ian as drum roadie and sound man, Liam, who lifted Geddy's equipment and called lights, and Dave Scace who worked as guitar roadie for a few weeks, soon to be replaced by J.J. Johnson.

Howard took over the lighting after a couple of shows. Liam never had enough time to look after them properly, and Howard was glad to take the job off his hands. One of the reasons for the change was all the new equipment. "The first show we did with Uriah Heep was with almost entirely new gear," Liam says. "There was no chance to work any of the bugs out at all. So the first few weeks were frantic. It was a matter of ploughing through and persevering as well as we could, and we pulled it off."

Alex, Geddy and Neil travelled by car with Howard. Ian, Liam and J.J used a 12-foot G.M.C. box truck to cart around the equipment and themselves. Within a few weeks, Neil began to feel like a member of the band, instead of just a last-minute replacement. His drumming skills added to the band's sound. He was soon able to give them a tightness they never had with John. "The songs were the same, but with Neil they had a different treatment," says Alex. "A really good feeling was established between us."

Once the equipment problems were sorted out, the band and crew found they had plenty of free time on their hands. Since they were an opening act, they rarely played for more than half an hour, and there was not that much set-up time, since the headliner brought the lights and sound system. Often Rush had no time for a sound check if the main act decided it needed to tune up. It was very different from playing five or six hours a night in Toronto bars.

While the crew used the extra time to see the US, the band spent hours writing new material. According to Alex much of the work was done "sitting in hotel rooms, writing heavy metal tunes on acoustic guitars."

The long hours of travelling between gigs may have been hard on a more experienced group, but for the members of Rush, their first major tour was a dream come true. "It was so exciting," says Alex. "You couldn't wait for the next day to start. Travelling . . . going where I never thought I would go. We all felt like that. It was a little rough on the back, travelling by car, but we could deal with it."

On one of those rent-a-car runs, 'Making Memories' was written with Alex in the front seat strumming on a guitar. The song captures the time. 'There's a time for feeling as good as we can/ The time is now and there's no stopping us.'

But no matter how enjoyable the tour was, there were at least some memories in the making that did not seem funny at the time. The band had just played St. Louis. Howard pointed the car, which was engulfed in pot smoke, in what he thought was the direction of Cleveland. Three hours into the trip as they neared Memphis, Tennessee, Howard realised he was going in the opposite direction and it was no time to stop by and meet Elvis. Alex, Geddy's and Neil's singing turned into screaming. In response, Howard turned the car around and tore off to Evansville, Indiana where the band could catch a plane. They pulled into the airport parking lot just in time to see the Delta jet 'fly by night' departing.

Rush opened for many bands during the tour. Besides Uriah Heep they warmed up the crowd for Rory Gallagher, Hawkwind, Blue Oyster Cult, Nazareth, Kiss, P.F.M., Billy Preston, Wet Willie, The Marshall Tucker Band and Manfred Mann. Gallagher always treated the band well, and in later years Rory would open many a show for them.

Rush also played a handful of headlining gigs in small clubs. At these dates the trio would play most of the first album and several early songs from their bar band days like, 'Fancy Dancer' and 'Garden Road' along with a few cover songs done à la Rush.

In September the band recorded a Toronto concert that was aired on The King Biscuit Flower Hour. On October 9, 1974, the trio taped a Don Kirshner's Rock Concert. Neil broke a bass drum head during the shooting of 'Best I Can' on ABC Television's In Concert series. That was aired on December 6, 1974. The band also appeared on quite a few local television shows during the period.

Just before Christmas Cliff Burnstein set up an important radio concert for the group in New York City. Rush's gear was set up in Jimi Hendrix's Electric Ladyland Studios. The show was broadcast live over WQIV to Big Apple rock fans.

Cliff hoped that the concert would help break the band in New York. They had received very little airplay in the States' largest city, but if the band could get a following in the media capital of the country, success in the smaller towns would be easier to achieve. For, despite heavy touring and that initial burst of airplay in Cleveland, radio was a shaky proposition for Rush. The strategy, according to Ray was "If you were not a hit singles act, you had to tour. So that's where we started and as a result of where we played we'd end up at least getting token airplay. Record sales would go with it. We just built up territory by territory. Rush almost never received airplay before they played in a town."

Besides giving the group radio time in New York, the show gives a good sound picture of the band, just a few months after Neil joined and before they hit the studio for the second album. The guys played much of the first album, along with Larry Williams' '50s rock song (covered by The Beatles) 'Bad Boy'. Several tunes from 'Fly By Night' made an early appearance. 'Anthem' sounds much as it did on the record, but the title track is very different. Part of 'By-Tor And The Snowdog' is tacked on to the end of 'Fly By Night'.

Even at this early date you can hear the power of Peart's drumming. Geddy's singing is loose. He hasn't learned all the lines to the new songs, and he does not have the control over his voice he was later to attain. Alex sings back-up on 'Best I Can'. His guitar work is sharp. As an ensemble the group's playing is a little rough around the edges. Still, there is a powerful passion to their performance.

With much of what would become the second album already written, it was time to head back to the recording studio. Neil had taken over most of the lyric writing. Neither Geddy nor Alex really took to lyric writing, so when Neil began writing, the pair encouraged him. "Gedd and I weren't into it," says Alex. "On the first album Gedd wrote most of the lyrics, all but one song ('Here Again'). With 'Fly By Night' we figured if Neil wanted to do it, fine. Especially since when you're writing music it's difficult for a drummer to take a strong hand in the melodic writing of a song. So Gedd and I did that and Neil took over the lyrics."

The first Rush song with lyrics penned by Peart was 'Fly By Night'. He had worked on a few songs before he joined the band, but he became the lyric writer for Rush by default. "Basically it was because nobody else wanted to do it," says Neil. "And I thought, well, I've always been interested in words. I've always loved to read. So why not give it a try. I wrote a couple of songs and showed them to Alex and Geddy. They liked them. So I continued. It later became an obsession."

The material for 'Fly By Night' was formulated during the period Alex, Geddy and Neil were really becoming acquainted with each other. A chemistry was starting to develop between the three that had not existed when John left the band. "We were pooling our creative resources," Neil later wrote, "and exploring each other's aptitudes and personal ities. A real unity of purpose was beginning to develop."

In many ways it was a different band assembled in Toronto for 'Fly By Night'. Neil's effect on Alex and Geddy and their effect on him would cause a burst in their collective creativity.

Terry Brown was once again behind the board. For Terry, the second album, recorded and mixed in 10 days, was, "A bit of a panic... but we made it. In those days it was strange because you had nothing really to judge it by. All we knew were the tunes and the direction we wanted. So it was just a question of working ridiculous hours. I mean you just start with day one and make it to day two, and so on. There was no discussion of 'Is it okay', 'Do we need to remix anything', or 'Would you have rather done this or that'. When it was done, that was it. There was no time for discussion when the album was finished. We rushed out, cut it and pressed it."

No matter what the time constraints, just the fact that they were getting a chance to record a second album signalled to the band that they had staying power. As it turned out, a lot more than they could have ever imagined.

Hectic understates the last minute nature of the way the record was completed. Alex said, "It was 8 o'clock in the morning, and we had just finished mixing when Vic Wilson came down to pick up the tapes. We had worked most of the previous day and night and then on the final night straight through until the morning. After all this we went to the airport to catch a 10.30am flight to Winnipeg for a gig. We were so tired we barely made it to the airport. I remember sleeping for an hour and a half on the plane, getting there, waking up, and it was freezing cold. We had a horrible day. It was snowing and it felt like minus 580 degrees. I'll never forget trying to get it together in the dressing room before the show. A crazy day."

The hard work resulted in a large step forward for the band. Putting aside for a moment the songs themselves, the playing sounded as if the revamped

Gary and Alex at Fisherville Junior High School.

trio had been together for years, not months. Neil was already showing that he was a great rock drummer but the improvements were across the board. Before, the distortion had covered up the fact that only three people were playing, now it was the group's chops that did the trick. All three shared leads and rhythms. Geddy and Alex's trademark bass and guitar riffs are in full evidence. Even with Neil's first appearance on vinyl, he has his own style. You can hear the manic fury of a Keith Moon, but there is an added control that is strictly Neil Peart. 'Fly By Night' showed that the three musicians could sound like five or six.

The straightforward, hard rock of the first album was still there. Yet it was tighter and more focused. Quieter passages were brought to life by Geddy and Alex's playing of acoustic guitars. Neil's battery of percussion toys brought new textures to many of the songs. In comparison to 'Rush', 'Fly By Night' is almost symphonic rock.

The album opens with 'Anthem', a tough tune with tough subject matter. Neil had interested the other members of the band in the philosophy of 'objectivist' writer Ayn Rand, and the title is taken from a novella of the same name in which Rand wrote about a world where individual initiative is forbidden, and all is done collectively. To Rand, this was the ultimate horror. Having experienced the Russian Revolution in 1917 at first hand, she believed that all of man's great achievements were accomplished by individuals and that collective actions were often destructive; in many cases destructive of society's most outstanding figures. To the band her uncompromising position was a model for many years for it seemed to mirror their determination to do things their own way. Paradoxically Rand would probably have been horrified by the group. Although they went their own way, they did so collectively, and Rand railed against long-haired hippies and rock music on several occasions, most notably in a collection of essays on the Woodstock Generation.

'Best I Can' comes next, a Geddy/Lee rock composition like 'Beneath, Between And Behind' which follows.

'By-Tor And The Snowdog' marks the beginning of a Rush tradition of extended story songs, in this case a battle between By-Tor and the Snowdog. The song has bite, in more ways than one. Howard actually came up with the title one night at a party at Ray's house. "Ray had these two dogs," says Howard. "One was a German Shepherd that had these fangs, and the other was this little tiny white nervous dog. I used to call the Shepherd By-Tor

Geddy with the Fender
Precision bass before it
was remodelled into the
teardrop shape.

because anyone who would walk into the house would get bitten by him. Ray would go, 'This dog is trained fine, don't worry about it.' Well the night of the party we were sitting down eating our steaks when the Shepherd started biting my leg. I started screaming and calling the dog a By-Tor. Now the other dog was real neurotic, constantly barking and jumping all over you. And since he was a snow dog, I started calling the pair 'By-Tor and the Snowdog'."

The second side opens on a high note with 'Fly By Night', a really potential hit single, followed by 'Making Memories', a tune which captures Rush's early experiences on the road. Next is 'Rivendell', inspired by the ever-popular J.R.R. Tolkien, whose tales inspired a series of early '70s rockers including Led Zeppelin. 'Rivendell' is the name of a city of elves

mentioned in the Lord of the Rings trilogy and other works by Tolkien, a paradise on earth. Geddy's keening vocals suggest the beauty this imaginary refuge had for him and Neil. Incidentally, Tolkien's influence could also be heard on 'By-Tor And The Snowdog' and several later songs by the band.

The album closer, 'In The End' opens quietly, much like 'Rivendell'. But then Alex kicks in with a killer guitar riff followed by Neil and Geddy before a classic Rush tempo change.

'Fly By Night' hit the record racks in February 1975. By that time the band were already back on the road, opening shows for Kiss and Aerosmith, with the occasional headlining gig on the side.

The dates with Kiss were particularly memorable. Kiss were on their way to becoming one of

Neil with Peter Criss
of Kiss.

rock's biggest bands. Their mixture of extreme theatrics, painted faces and bone crushing hard rock made them a tough act to precede. Their fans expected a spectacle and Rush managed to hold their own. The members of Kiss were friendly to Alex, Geddy and Neil, and much fun was had on their tour.

Gene Simmons, the long-tongued bassist of Kiss, said "We've always had great bands open for us. We believe in exposing good talent to the people. We liked Rush for their Led Zeppelin junior approach. Very straightforward kick-ass rock."

Neil described the final show Rush played with Kiss to a writer from *Circus* magazine. The date was in San Diego. "We were going to dress up as them, put on their make-up, and go out and do our set as them, but what finally happened was an onstage pie-fight that happened in front of 6,000 screaming kids. They caught us at the end of our set by surprise, and the whole stage was covered in shaving cream and whipped cream. Then it was our turn at the end of their set. All their guitars and drums and machines were completely buried in shaving cream, so their encore sounded just great!" "The end of tour party," said Geddy, "was one of those great all-nighters with stuff being thrown out of the hotel windows."

In between tour dates Alex married his long-time girlfriend, Charlene, on March 12, 1975. They had been seeing each other since Alex was 15. The honeymoon was a little unconventional. "On our honeymoon," says Charlene, "he was playing up north and I had to go by myself. He had a couple of shows to do, so he came down and met me later. I thought, hmmm! This is a sign of what it is going to be like (laughter)."

Also around this time Ray wanted to change the name of Moon Records. Rush made some suggestions and eventually they came up with the title and theme of Anthem so he used it as the new name for the company. He also liked it because Anthem sounded like a great name for a record company. "It was tied in with Rush but it didn't mean we couldn't put another act on the label," says Ray.

The second tour saw the band begin to pick up pockets of loyal fans across the United States. The gigging paid off with limited airplay, mainly in the Midwest, where the band began to sell out small gigs as a headliner. While Rush were treated very well by Kiss, not every group they opened for was so kind.

On April 13, the trio played a sold-out show in front of 4,500 fans at Detroit's Michigan Palace. Another show at the Agora in Cleveland was a tour highlight for Alex. "We ended up going to cities two or three times in the space of a year. In Cleveland we did

that show with ZZ Top. Then we came back and did one with Uriah Heep. We got a real strong response the second time around, so we were booked into the Agora two weeks later. It was a hot, sweaty, sold-out night. Lots of electricity."

Donna Halper was the stage announcer for the Agora show. "Rush had worked their way up from being the third act on the bill to the point where they could take an entire show themselves in Cleveland and just command the performance. Fans were fighting for tickets for days. The concert was then rebroadcast on WMMS."

While on tour with Aerosmith in Michigan the band received a phone call from a very drunk Ray Danniels. He was ranting and raving about Rush being the best new trio around. It took Alex, Geddy and Neil a few minutes before they realised what he was trying to say. Rush had won a Juno award for the most promising new group, the Canadian equivalent of the American Grammy Awards. The trio promptly went out and celebrated on their own. Rush had never won any kind of award before, so a few dozen drinks seemed to be in order.

The band closed the 'Fly By Night' tour with a short Canadian jaunt. But before they could begin the dates in their homeland there was the little matter of a rental car they had hired for the tour. They told the rental company they were only going to use it for a short period of time. Eventually it was returned a few months later with 11,000 additional miles on the clock, no hubcaps, no rear-view mirror and a broken radio. Alex later told David Fricke in an article for *Rolling Stone* magazine that the vehicle was ruined. And that the people at the rental agency "were quite surprised."

On June 25, Massey Hall in Toronto held 2,765 Rush fans as the band blasted their way through a sold out show. Max Webster warmed the crowd. Alex was blown away by the way the fans seemed to know the words to every song. Neil could hardly believe he was playing at Massey Hall. He had always dreamed of playing at the venue and there he was pounding away as part of a successful rock band, and in top form too. His solo spot utilised speaker panning and a phase shifter that filtered the sound of his snare. To Geddy it was the culmination of seven years of hard work.

'Fly By Night' was out-selling the first album and was not unheard of on radio. The second half of 1975 would see a longer album, extended songs, more complex arrangements and lyrics, constant concerts and a serious testing of Alex, Geddy and Neil's commitment to make music their own way.

*t*he Three Men Of Willowdale' returned to Toronto Sound in July of 1975 to begin work on their third album. Terry Brown was once again producing. With the success of the first two efforts, the band were in a confident mood, and their steadily increasing popularity had heightened the trio's resolve. In Neil's words it "helped to reinforce our belief in what we were trying to accomplish, and we became dedicated to achieving success without compromising our music, for we felt that it would be worthless on any other terms."

As with 'Fly By Night' most of 'Caress Of Steel' was written on the road. The new material was a real stretch for the band and with only 12 days budgeted for the recording and mixing of the record, it would prove difficult to get the sound they wanted down on tape.

The main factor in their favour was that much of the material had been worked out beforehand. Alex remembers how the album's musical and lyrical patterns were developed. "Neil wrote the lyrics for the 'Fountain Of Lamneth'," says Alex, "and he thought it would be kind of nice to try to incorporate a very loose concept in it, by having a starting point, and an ending point, which would cover a whole album side. It would be a complete story but broken up so that they could be taken as individual songs, that unless you looked closely wouldn't necessarily relate to each other. That was how we approached it. It was also important for us to continue the By-Tor thing on the album with a piece that was eventually titled 'The Necromancer'."

But the band had bitten off more than they could chew. The time and care needed to work on such a complex undertaking was not possible with less than two weeks in the studio. In retrospect Terry agrees with this assessment, referring to the album as an ambitious project that did not quite come off. According to Terry, the production is too loose, and a few more weeks of work would have solved many problems. But he thinks that the musical ideas were very strong. Still, the record is probably the first where Rush were conscious of developing an original

Return of the prince – Rush against the world.

sound. While they do not quite achieve their own sound, they go quite a way towards doing so. The sessions laid a firm musical base for what was to follow.

The album begins with a bang, with 'Bastille Day' one of the finest hard rock songs ever recorded. It is a song of the French Revolution with music to match angry words, reaching new levels of complexity and ambiguity. Clearly influenced by Charles Dickens' riveting description of the terror in 'A Tale Of Two Cities', Neil expresses both the savagery of the mob, and the reasons for its behaviour. While at other times in the band's career Neil's mistrust of people acting en masse would bring out a palpable loathing of such collective action, on this song you can't quite tell which side he is on. This impression is reinforced by Geddy's passionate vocal After all, the band now had the experience of playing in front of thousands of excited people and seen both the positive and negative aspects of communal experiences.

A complete change of pace follows. 'I Think I'm Going Bald' opens with an echoed shriek from Geddy that sounds as if he has just seen what he is about to describe. It is about waking up, looking in the mirror and thinking that you are going bald. The song has an amusing closing lyrical prophecy; 'But even when I'm grey I'll still be grey my way.'

'Lakeside Park' evokes lazy summer days and nights. The kind of life that the band had given up in order to 'make it'. Geddy's vocal has a poignancy that shows that at least part of him misses those carefree days. It's the kind of song to which just about every listener can relate because most of us have a Lakeside Park of our own.

Next comes a continuation of 'By-Tor And The Snowdog' in 'The Necromancer'. The strangest introductory vocal about 'three travellers, men of Willowdale' was created by treating Neil's voice with special effects using a digital delay unit and slowing the recording speed. It expands on the tentative art rock experiments of 'Fly By Night'. A whole bevy of effects are employed to heighten the sonic experience of the piece, or actually pieces. 'The Necromancer' is really three movements strung together as

one, united by the battle between By-Tor and the Necromancer. The song shares with several tunes from the previous album a heavy J.R.R. Tolkien influence with its talk of wizards, wraiths and tower fortresses. It is also the first time Rush extended a concept from one LP to another.

The second half of the album contains Rush's first side-long composition. On the cover of the record, six individual songs are listed, but even a casual listen reveals they are meant to be taken as a whole. There are several recurring musical and lyrical motifs, and the tracks all melt into each other. The epic appears to be about a man's compulsion to see and taste the world, and if possible to understand what these experiences mean. The traveller finds that the key, the end, the answer, is that there is none. The suite's highlights, a drum showcase for Neil on 'Didacts And Narpets', 'Bacchus Plateau', 'The Fountain' and 'No One At The Bridge'.

Even with the strict time limits, you can hear how the band is developing its compositional skills. The playing is solid with definite signs of improvement, but it is not as noticeable as the leaps in technique made from the first to the second album. As events turned out, 'Caress Of Steel' would come in for quite a drubbing, but the record, if far from perfect, contains much of what Rush would become, and more than

that stands up today as a whole, something that only parts of 'Rush' and 'Fly By Night' achieve. As a matter of fact, just like the first record it has a small, but devoted band of fans who think it is the best thing Rush have ever done. Although critical of his own production, Terry Brown is one of those who 'loves' the record.

Rush played down the disc in later years, but Terry says that, "At the time they were very happy with it. Not many others shared this view. Right from the beginning it was not going to be a very big record (laugh), everyone who heard it sort of went 'Um, yes, oh, a new direction'. From an outsider's point of view it was very difficult to get into 'Caress' quickly. But there are some great tunes on it."

Neil talked about the attitude of the band while they were recording the album. "We went in serene and confident, and emerged with an album that we were tremendously proud of, as a major step in our development, and featuring a lot of dynamic variety and some true originality."

Rush were set for their third tour with an album that they thought would win over more fans and garner more airplay. Although there were warning signs from the reactions of those around them, the band were convinced that they had not only pleased themselves, but had also gone another big step towards establishing themselves as a definite entity. They were in for an upsetting surprise.

When it came to designing the cover, another contributor to the band's look and sound arrived on the scene. Hugh Syme, a member of the Ian Thomas Band also on Anthem Records, had previously asked to design one of the Thomas album covers. Ray agreed, liked his work and asked him to come up with some ideas for the 'Caress' packaging. Hugh made pencil drawings of a man on a mountain with a floating pyramid at his front, and a snake by his side. The group's name was above the picture. The title of the album was below it. When the jackets were printed, the colour separation people botched the job, much as they had with the first album. Hugh's rather striking idea of doing the front cover in a glaring steel tone was translated to a brass or copperish colour. Since the new colour had nothing to do with steel, the entire cover concept was ruined. By the time the band saw what had happened hundreds of thousands of the fold-out covers had been printed and it would have been too expensive at this stage in Rush's career to reprint them. It was an omen for what was to come.

The album, complete with a dedication to Rod Serling, came out in September 1975. 'Return Of The Prince' from 'The Necromancer' was released as the

single. It died, and the album itself moved off the shelves very slowly. Rush received no radio airplay from 'Caress Of Steel'.

Terry knew the lack of radio play was a sign of trouble. "I guess the band didn't have quite the pull airplay wise. We never have," said Broon. "It's always been a problem. If you make a record that's on the other side of it, then you can forget the airplay. 'Caress Of Steel' was a prime example. It wasn't accessible enough for radio to get into." These radio programmers obviously didn't have the compact disc version of 'Caress Of Steel'. Released in March 1987, remastered from the original tapes, it is worth the price of buying a disc player just to hear this highly underrated recording.

As the band embarked on its three-and-a-half month 'Caress Of Steel' tour their high spirits began to sag, although one positive development was a slight improvement in their travelling conditions. Instead of a rental car, the trio travelled in a Funcraft Van, complete with a small refrigerator and four sleeping bunks, which was nicknamed 'The Blue Rocket'. The crew consisted of Howard acting as road manager and lighting director, Ian with double duties as drum technician and sound man, Liam switched from bass roadie to guitar technician, and newcomer Skip Gildersleeve who replaced Jim Johnson. He met the band during their appearances at Detroit's Michigan Palace.

Everyone shared the driving chores. Skip explains how it worked. "We had a driving rotation schedule, where Neil would write this sheet out (there was a three-man crew, not including Howard) so you would be up to drive one night, the next night you were back-up driver, the night after that you rode with the band and you didn't have to drive at all. The band and Howard had the same schedule with the Funcraft."

As word filtered back from the record company on the disappointing sales of 'Caress Of Steel' the band also got the message from falling audience attendance and enthusiasm. While Rush could feel the momentum building on the first two tours, this was not the case on the third. Band and crew began only half-jokingly calling it 'The Down The Tubes Tour'. And as the jaunt progressed the smiles got rarer.

According to Neil it "was a pretty depressing string of small towns and small clubs." Everyone was disappointed. Liam recalled, "I expected it to be a much larger album and tour. They just weren't getting the acceptance they deserved. Looking back on it maybe the album was a little self-indulgent, but I thought the material was extremely good and couldn't understand why it wasn't being accepted. Maybe it wasn't commercial enough for the audience."

Things got so grim, as Geddy later told *Guitar Player* magazine, there was a moment "when we thought 'well maybe we should just hang it up and go home.' I remember we were on an overnight drive to Atlanta, Georgia and we were all real depressed, saying 'Oh this is never going to work! What are we doing here?'"

As 1975 and 'The Down The Tubes Tour' ground to a close, the band's very name seemed to be an ironic comment on their lack of progress. With a decline in record sales, they began to have problems with their cash flow. Ray Danniels was $325,000 in the hole with Rush with only an ulcer to show for it. For weeks at a time they were not paid their regular touring salaries. On each occasion the cheques stopped, they wondered whether or not it was for good. Alex said, "We didn't know what to do, we were not sure what direction to take."

But others were more than ready to offer advice. Record company executives and the band's management began to express doubts about the course Rush were taking, and even their future prospects. Unwanted and unsolicited outside suggestions came flooding in.

Talk of hit singles, and a return to a Led Zeppelin Junior approach were frequent. The band had to make a crucial choice. "We had worked very, very hard," said Alex, "and all of a sudden we weren't getting any support. By the nature of the way our deal was set up at the record company we had freedom to do musically what we wanted. When after 'Caress' there was that lack of support . . . we had to decide whether we were going to say . . . okay, we give up. We either break up, or we try to make another first album, or we say fuck it and do whatever we want. We decided on the third choice. We talked about the whole thing, and got really fired up between the three of us to really push on and not worry about what anyone else thought."

Their determination was bolstered by an idea Neil was working on. His continuing fascination with Ayn Rand was to provide him with a concept that would push the trio to come up with a finished product that matched their promise. Rand's depictions of heroic men and women fighting for their creative freedom against a hostile society took on an even more personal meaning for the group. Neil saw a parallel between Rand's characters and Rush's struggles.

Conceived in bits and pieces during 'The Down The Tubes Tour', the material showed a new maturity in Neil's writing. His lyrics show an economy of expression that he had achieved only sporadically before. By the time the piece took its final shape it concerned a time in the not too distant future when a galaxy-wide war results in the rule of all the planets by

Across the Styx.

a caste of priests who maintain control through a massive system of computers. All art and expression is channelled through the computers into a bland unified whole.

One man in this future-gone-awry accidentally rediscovers a guitar, slowly teaches himself to play the instrument and gradually learns that he can make music by himself. A music that expresses his individuality and implicitly rejects the orthodoxy of the priests. The man, only wishing to do good, rushes to tell his rulers of the discovery. The priests listen to the new music and tell him it has no place in their world. The hero returns dejected to the place where he found the guitar. He then falls asleep and dreams that an oracle shows him the way to paradise. When he awakes, the man realises that the beauty he has seen was only a dream. After several days' reflection, he comes to the conclusion that he cannot continue. So he takes his own life, with the hope of moving on to a better one. Then in Neil's words, "As he dies another planetary battle begins - with the outcome to be determined in the mind of the listener."

Alex and Geddy quickly saw how Neil's concept related to their own problems. It inspired them to go for a tighter, more focused sound. Whereas on 'Caress Of Steel' you could still hear echoes of Rush's influences, the new material gave them a sound they could call their own.

Neil later wrote about the period. "It was uncertain for a time whether we would fight or fall, but finally we got mad! We came back with a vengeance . . . we were talking about freedom from tyranny and *meant* it. This was the first real blend of our diverse and schizophrenic influences."

Geddy said the piece was a combination of everything the band wanted to say at the time. He said Rush were trying to say musically what Ayn Rand had expressed on the printed page. "When Neil came up with the lyrics," said Geddy, "we worked out the music over an extended period of time. The philosophy we have as a band just came out."

This can be heard at the very start of the piece. There is the sound of what appears to be a spacecraft landing. Then the band kicks in. Alex rips into his guitar. A thick bass line and pounding drums join in as Rush embark on their most aggressive, and yet at the same time controlled, musical journey to that date. Rush's frustration and the theme of the material are inseparable. Then there is an explosion followed by a sudden calm in the musical storm as Geddy softly sings, 'And the meek shall inherit the earth.'

The fury of the opening suddenly returns with Geddy lashing out in his fantastic falsetto: 'We've taken care of everything/ The words you read/ The songs you sing/ The pictures that give pleasure to your eyes/ One for all/ And all for one/ Work together common sons/ Never need to wonder how or why.'

Contained in those lyrics and in the playing that accompanied them seemed to be a condemnation of all the compromises that others wanted Rush to make.

The band road tested the new material during the final leg of 'The Down The Tubes Tour' in order to work out as much of the piece as possible before recording. There was no better way to do it than in front of a live audience.

Even though the band was regaining some of its lost confidence, the trio had no way of knowing whether their next record would be any more successful than 'Caress Of Steel'. In fact they were wary of their own judgement, because they had such high hopes for the third album. But the conflict had succeeded in unleashing the creative power of the band more than they knew, and the extensive pre-production work put the members of Rush in the best position they had ever been in prior to recording an album. Now the only problem was getting '2112' on tape.

*a*s Rush prepared to head into the studio, they received some welcome news. *Circus* magazine readers picked the band as the second best new group for 1975, a confidence builder which would help to bolster the trio's growing sense that they would stand or fall on their own terms.

The biggest lesson the band had learned from 'Caress' was that if they were going to try more ambitious material, they would need more than a week or two of recording time. With the new songs they had spent a six-month period intermittently writing while on the road and they wanted the finished product to reflect their intense involvement in the piece. So a full month was set aside to record and mix the album with Broon at Toronto Sound.

There were several other important decisions made about the album. Since Rush were above all a touring band, they wanted to be able to reproduce the new songs live. At the same time they wanted to explore the full range of possibilities available to them in the studio. The trio decided they would use as few overdubs as possible on most of the record, but they would set one track aside for some studio research where they could create like crazy, without worrying about having to reproduce it live.

The recording went well. Both Broon and the band were happy with the initial results. But Terry later admitted he had no idea how well the album would do. "I wasn't really sure where '2112' would go in so far as overall (commercial) success," said Terry. "I find it very hard to make a judgement. If you had asked me then, I would have said that 'Caress Of Steel' and '2112' were very much in the same area as far as success ratings go."

On the title track, two bits of studio magic helped to give the band some extra gloss. Hugh Syme and Geddy played an ARP synthesizer at the start of the piece. The effect was achieved in one take creating feedback with an envelope generator. Terry then treated it with echo and reverb.

The eerie voice that closes out 'Grand Finale' by assuming control was actually created long before the '2112' session. "It was at the end of 'Caress Of Steel'

Neil, Alex and Geddy with their wives.

We have assumed control.

when we got a digital delay unit in the studio," remembered Terry. "This little black box kept us entertained for a whole night (laughs) and we recorded about two rolls of tape. Much of it was the four of us being very silly. We came up with a lot of good ideas, and also found out exactly how this thing worked, and what its potential was. One thing we came up with was the voice for the finale. So we saved the tape, and pulled it out when we did '2112'."

Hugh Syme's contributions to the album were not limited to a synthesizer effect. He once again made an important graphic contribution to the band's image and played on the album, the first time an outsider played on a Rush record. He worked on the studio production 'Tears'. On the song he filled up three tracks with Mellotron parts, mimicking strings, a French horn and flutes. Hugh's cover design would actually serve as the group's trademark for many years to come. He began to devise the concept for the artwork even before the record was finished, getting a copy of the lyrics and some of the music and talking with the trio about the general direction of the album. He then went to work.

The front cover features a painting of the galaxy with the band's name and title on it. Underneath the title is a red star inside a circle. The jacket has a gatefold design. When the cover is opened, the right side reveals the album's lyrics in red. The left side has a drawing of a naked man holding his hands out in front of him to ward off the star. This image intrigued the band and it eventually became their logo for almost a decade.

In later years, some foolish people tried to attach a satanic meaning to the design because of the red colour, the pentagram-like shape of the star, and circle.

Hugh explained to *Creem* magazine that, "This man is the hero of the story. That he is nude is just a classical tradition . . . the pureness of his person and creativity without the trappings of other elements such as clothing. The red star is the evil red star of the federation, which was one of Neil's symbols. We basically based that cover around that red star and the hero." The result according to Geddy was something that "to us came to stand for individualism or man against the masses."

That symbol perfectly represented what Rush were trying to achieve on '2112'. It caught not only the ambience of the title piece, but also the more conventional tracks on the second side of the record.

Side Two opens with 'A Passage To Bangkok', a song about a fantasy journey to the finest marijuana fields in the world and obviously the work of a T-H-C connoisseur.

There is another nod to the man 'Caress Of Steel' was dedicated to on 'The Twilight Zone'. It has a mystical space feel, and I think Rod Serling would have loved it. 'Lessons' is a rarity in that Alex gets the sole songwriting credit. But in another sense, it is an atypical Rush song, opening quietly before rocking out. Next is the studio production piece, 'Tears'. Although better produced, it is very much in the mode of 'Rivendell'. The song also marks one of the very few times that Neil plays in a straight four-time signature.

The album closes with perhaps the clearest and most concise statement of purpose the band ever recorded. 'Something For Nothing' sounds like a call to action. 'You don't get something for nothing/ You don't get freedom for free/ You won't get wise/ With the sleep still in your eyes/ No matter what your dream might be.'

The album as a whole is much better produced than their earlier efforts, and really shines on compact disc.

When the band delivered the finished product to Mercury, the record company executives were furious. Here was a hard rock act that had gone 'arty' on their last album. The record had flopped, and what did they do, but go in and make an even artier disc. To top things off, Rush wanted a 20 minute cut to lead-off the album. Their contract gave them artistic control which meant Mercury could not move the song to the second side of the record.

Only a handful of people at the label took the band's side. Cliff Burnstein lobbied hard telling company brass that unlike the last album, '2112' had the extra polish that could put the band over commercially, but most of his colleagues strongly disagreed.

Even Terry had his doubts. "It didn't seem to me that '2112' would be that much bigger," he says, "but everything was a bit more together. The album cover was more positive, and attractive to the fan. 'Caress' had a very dark and gloomy cover, while the cover of '2112' is quite stunning."

The record was released in March 1976 and the doubters at Mercury received a big surprise. Within a week of its release, 100,000 copies had been sold. The marketing plan had not even begun when orders for more records began pouring in. By the end of the month, sales surpassed the first three albums combined.

Rush played their first '2112' tour date in Los Angeles on March 18. Almost immediately after the album came out a difference was noticed by band and crew.

"To me it seemed to be the big turning point," said Liam. "Obviously everyone felt like they were under a lot of pressure. If you have an album that stiffs, the pressure is that much greater for the next album to be that much better. '2112' was accepted extremely well. It was a day and night difference between 'Caress Of Steel' and '2112'. It was a good thing too, because there were a lot of down feelings on 'The Down The Tubes Tour' and things turned around completely with '2112' so it was very uplifting."

After playing on the West coast, Rush moved to their strongest area, the American Midwest where they had spent much time touring and it was beginning to pay off.

"We started headlining small places on the 'Caress' tour," says Alex, "and we didn't really do that well in the majority of the halls. With '2112' it seemed to change. We would go back to these same

halls and do a lot better. In many cities we were going the next step up the ladder, headlining 5,000 seat arenas."

This popularity came from playing places like St. Louis where they did four shows within an 18 month period. Rush were now playing a total of more than 300 shows every year, mostly one night stands. Another change was when they were billed as an opening act, they were often called 'Special Guests'. By May the group was playing a series of dates across Texas stages to prepare for the album that would sum up their development. Rush were getting ready to record a live album.

The idea made perfect sense for the trio. Much of their success came from playing live. Even radio airplay came only after Rush had visited an area. Plus an in-concert package would be welcomed by their fans. There were also more practical reasons: Alex, Geddy and Neil had exhausted themselves working on '2112'. They needed time to figure out what their next musical direction would be. A live set would buy them an extra six months. It would also (theoretically) be easier to produce.

King Lerxst.

1976 was the year of the live album. Former tour mates Kiss were well on the way to becoming one of the biggest rock bands in America as a result of the 'Kiss Alive' record. The same thing was happening to a hitherto obscure British guitar player by the name of Peter Frampton, and a perennial Detroit local hero Bob Seger who was stirring up interest with his 'Live Bullet' package, not to mention Lynyrd Skynyrd, Foghat and Led Zeppelin.

With a live album a natural next step, choosing a site was even easier. Toronto would be the place. Two dates were booked at Massey Hall, which would also serve as the kick-off to a brief Canadian tour. Tickets for the first two shows sold out immediately. A third show was added and all tickets for that date were also sold.

Rush had been performing an energetic spirited live set for three full months when they hit the stage at Massey Hall on June 11.

As Skip Gildersleeve cried out, "Oh . . . won't you please welcome home Rush," Terry was watching the dials in the Fedco mobile recording truck. "Other than freaking out and trying to get it all together, I don't remember anything about the shows. It was a bit of a nightmare to me," Terry says.

The pressure was on everyone. "Hometown is always intense," says Liam, "much more so than any other gigs. Everyone wants to be at their best playing to a hometown audience. Add to that the fact that we were recording a live album, it was extremely high

pressure for a few days. It felt like we were there for weeks."

To Alex, "Three days at Massey Hall was a big deal. It was something to be really proud of, for us, being a Toronto band, and coming home and having that kind of response. We still got a lot of bad press about those shows, but that made it even better."

The first two nights' performances were good, and the band were counting on a magical show on the third. At the time, Rush always played best on their third straight show. The trio found that the first two dates put them in peak form, and the third was an occasion for a trip into the upper stratosphere.

So when they hit the stage for the final night's performance, all concerned knew that every note had to count. But they ran into problems, Neil especially, as he later told Jim Ladd on the syndicated radio show, *Innerview*. "I had a lot of equipment troubles . . . and I was just burning with rage . . . because there is no time . . . when you respond emotionally like you do onstage . . . everything just (snaps his fingers) . . . you respond spontaneously. I never lose my temper except when I'm on stage . . . because

when things go wrong there . . . I'm wide open emotionally . . . . because of what I'm involved in . . . the level of concentration . . . I don't have time for a rational response . . . I just go urrrgghh.

"So consequently all of this angst was coming out of me during the course of the night, and I was so annoyed, and I figured the album was ruined because of all this. And then we listened back to those tapes and those were the ones that had all the energy, and it's true that anger can sometimes bring out the passion in the music."

As it turned out most of the two record set was taken from the third night's fiery performance. But, perhaps, what was most surprising to Terry and the band was how long it took to get the raw tapes ready for release. Everyone involved thought it would take a few days, and could be done right after the Canadian Tour. Then the band would be able to have a month to relax with their friends and families. It was not to be.

"We remixed the entire album three times", says Alex. "We thought it would take a week, maybe five days . . . and we were in there for a month. Geddy, Neil and I were going nuts by the end of it. We would

Recording in Massey Hall, without bass drum heads.

go outside and play ping- pong, go back in for a few minutes and walk out. We got to the point where we did not know what we were hearing any more. We tried to get a balance between a very live album and the way we would want to hear it."

Geddy told Toronto's *Globe and Mail* newspaper during the remixing of the record that some overdubbing was needed. He talked about fixing a guitar part that was ruined during 'Working Man' when Alex broke a string. But, Geddy was reluctant to talk about the dubbing process because he felt it would take away from the magic of the album. He did add that other well-known concert albums have had some studio wizardry performed on them.

Even with the occasional touch-up, the record sounds raw, catching the band's primal fury; an extra fire and energy that is missed on the studio versions. This is most notable on '2112'. Some of that intensity may come from Neil's anger, and if you listen closely you can hear the snares break on Neil's snare drum during 'The Temples Of Syrinx'. The live side of '2112' is also missing 'Oracle: The Dream'. While the band debuted this epic on tour, they were an opening act which meant that song sections were restricted due to time constraints, but as Rush began headlining they added the missing pieces back into '2112'. All of the pieces except for 'Oracle: The Dream' which has never been performed live. The album has definitive recordings of 'Bastille Day', 'Anthem', 'Something For Nothing', and of course, 'Working Man'.

The live album is also notable because it captures the band just as they were about to switch musical gears. Neil later said: "We look at a live album as taking the place of an anthology or greatest hits. To me it's a nicer way of doing that. It offers the high points of our material in a group of records, a span of our career, without just taking them off the albums."

Geddy found time off that summer to marry his long-time girlfriend, Nancy Young. The pair had a traditional Jewish wedding and were able to squeeze in a two-week Hawaiian honeymoon. Nancy had seen the band perform since its earliest days, and her brother Lindy was in Rush for a short time during 1969. Nancy and Geddy had been going out ever since.

'All The World's A Stage' was released September 29. Its title is the famed line from William Shakespeare's play, *As You Like It!*.

'All the world's a stage, and all the men and women merely players/They have their exits and entrances;and one man in his time plays many parts.'

North America would be Rush's stage for the remainder of 1976. A new tour started off with a few warm-up gigs in the United States, with a complex show that required a 10-man crew. A major highlight of the tour was their first appearance as headliners throughout Canada. Ray's strategy of breaking Rush in the US first left large areas of their homeland unexplored. Of course the band had always been popular in the Ontario area, but with their growing success, it seemed like the right time to alert the rest of the nation to Rush on stage.

All the new equipment was trucked into Canada. There were no problems at the border and all the gear cleared customs. However, on the eve of their first show at Moncton's Lewis Levesque Arena, the government stepped in, and they were slapped with a $15,000 fine for importing the equipment without a licence.

The tour itself had its share of failures. Attendance was spotty in the Maritime Provinces, and audiences were unresponsive. After the raucous atmosphere the band had been creating in the States and Toronto, the shows were a let-down. However, there was other news to cheer the group up. 'All The World's A Stage' was flying out of record stores. 215,000 copies of 'Stage' were shipped. '2112' was also still selling well. It had already passed the 300,000 mark and was continuing to move 5,000 copies a week. A much more enthusiastic Mercury Records reported that October was the best sales month in its 30 year history as a company. The new Rush release was a prime force in the sales explosion.

The band were soon back in the United States opening for Blue Oyster Cult. Geddy told the *Saginaw Michigan News* that the trio was going over well with stateside audiences. "It's good to see the response from an audience primarily interested in seeing the headliner," said Geddy. "We have got to the point where we are better able to select the kind of music we play to the kind of audience that shows up. I see a good future for the group." At that point, the band had played the Saginaw area three times in 12 months.

Geddy couldn't have known that the band would not have to tailor their show for other people's audiences much longer. As the tour progressed, Rush found themselves headlining more and more often. They even began to sell out medium sized halls of 5,000 to 7,000 seat capacity. The momentum was building. They also started touring extensively on the East Coast of the United States.

Until this period the trio had concentrated on the Midwest, and to a lesser degree on the West Coast. Their appearances along the Atlantic Seaboard had been few and far between. But, even as the third

billed act on the roster at coliseum concerts, Rush managed to make an impression and leave a few thousand fans behind in just about every city they visited.

It was a heady time for Alex, Geddy and Neil. They were beginning to be offered all the perks that come with being a successful rock band. Some were harmless, others were not.

On a lighter note, Neil reminisced about the first time the band played in Philadelphia. "I'll always remember the first time we played the Spectrum (where Rush opened for Robin Trower and Montrose). It was one of the very first times we had a limo, and we were talking with the stereo in the background. 'Still You Turn Me On' by ELP came on the radio while we talked together. It was a nice moment as we pulled up to the Spectrum."

On December 1 Rush opened for Ted Nugent at the L.A. Forum. Two weeks later they were back in Canada playing with Aerosmith at the Montreal Forum. On the 16th the trio sold out a 4,000 seat hall in Chicago. On December 22 they were presented Canadian Gold albums for 'Caress Of Steel' and 'Rush'. A Canadian Gold album is awarded for sales of 50,000 or more discs.

The band's dedication to science fiction and fantasy was also recognised when Marvel Comics dedicated The Defenders (Volume 1, Number 45) 'to Alex, Geddy and Neil of Rush'. The comic is based on Neil's lyrics to '2112'.

With things happening so fast it is a wonder that the band were also able to make a major decision about their future. The experiments of '2112' stimulated the group's appetite for musical change: they wanted to fully explore the progressive rock to which they had been listening and leaning towards for several years.

Since much of this music was keyboard orientated, the subject of expanding the group's line-up was broached for the first time since Mitch Bossi left. But one major factor stopped them: they had stood and succeeded as a trio. The lack of factions had always played in their favour. A unique chemistry had been formulated from this arrangement, and Alex and Geddy remembered the difficulties that always ensued when they added a fourth member. The idea was rejected.

Instead the band would work at expanding their instrumentation as a three-man unit. If, as Neil said, the live album summed up an era in the group's history, and a new road was to be taken, there would be at least one constant. Rush would consist only of the individuals who had risked everything to create

what was becoming a very distinct musical force.

New Year's Eve was celebrated with another hometown gig, a date at the Maple Leaf Gardens Concert Bowl. It was another big step up for the band in Toronto. All 7,000 seats were quickly sold out. This was a major achievement considering the group had played three nights at Massey Hall only seven months before. Gauging the response, Ray and Vic decided to go for a second show. It too sold out. Standing Room Only (SRO) Rush concerts would become an increasingly common phenomenon before the year was out. But by January 3 1977 two nights at the Concert Bowl were more than could be hoped for.

Even with this success, radio was still a problem. Rush got some airplay in the Midwest where their following was getting bigger all the time, but once outside this area radio was an invisible airwave for Rush, and even in the Midwest airplay tended to be closely tied to their concert appearances. Once they played a town, what little crackle of life they saw would taper off.

In Philadelphia a handful of songs made it onto the airwaves just before their first headlining gig at the Tower Theatre. But after the concert, that dwindled to nothing. Radio programmers seemed uninterested in slotting time for a group that was able to sell out a 3,500 seat hall, just a few months after being opening act on a triple bill.

Having just been converted to their music, I tried to do my bit by telling everyone I knew about Rush. I also started calling up the local stations and harassing disc jockeys, trying to get them to play the band's music. Among comments I heard: "Rush are raucous, they'll never make it," and "They are nothing more than a two-bit bar band." My continual phone calls

made me a few friends, a few enemies and even occasionally got Rush on the radio in Philadelphia.

The problems I encountered were much more frustrating for the band, its management and Mercury Records. They thought that the success of 'All The World's A Stage' and Rush's growing status as a touring band would open the airwaves to the trio. It didn't turn out that way. Rush continued to be pretty much non-existent as far as radio was concerned.

Cliff Burnstein was particularly annoyed. Since he had begun promoting the group he, "Kept on hitting brick walls with them. No airplay at major stations. The stations that did play Rush, however, got a response."

Cliff was always one to look for ways to blow up brick walls. He hit upon the idea of putting together a radio sampler of their work, collecting material from the post-Rutsey Rush albums. The disc included an edited version of '2112', 'Something For Nothing', 'Making Memories', and 'Bacchus Plateau'.

When it came to giving the package a title, Cliff decided to vent some of his frustration. He called it 'Everything Your Listeners Ever Wanted To Hear By Rush . . . But You Were Afraid To Play.' "It was aimed at people who would never put the group on their own turntables," says Cliff.

Rush carried on touring while Cliff and Mercury continued to batter away at the doors of US radio programmers. The band were using the time on the road to their advantage. They began working on new material, and learning to play new instruments during soundchecks.

"We thought we'd try and broaden the sound on stage between the three of us," says Alex, "by having Gedd play the keyboards and bass pedals, me playing bass pedals and double neck guitar, and Neil would get a few more percussion instruments to have some other sounds in there."

Armed with the incentive to keep the trio intact, their experiments soon began to produce results. The first song that used their new arsenal of equipment was 'Xanadu'. Work was started on it during the later stages of the 'All The World's A Stage Tour'. Among the instruments used, double neck guitars, bells, temple blocks, wind chimes, bass pedals and synthesizer. Other songs were also going through the writing process; 'Closer To The Heart' was completed and about half of 'Cygnus X-1' was finished.

North America's last look at Rush's stage for four months came in Chicago's Aragon Ballroom on May 20 and 21.

*t*he new chapter in the band's history would require other changes for Rush. Because the close proximity of friends and family had got in the way during the remixing of 'All The World's A Stage', the band decided that their next record would be made far away from the distractions of home life. Alex, Geddy and Neil would record the album in England, the home of art rock and the scene of Neil's first try at making it in the music business. Ray and Vic figured that as long as the group were overseas, they might as well schedule a two-week European tour. Dates were set in Great Britain, Sweden, Holland and West Germany.

In most of those countries Rush albums were being sold as imports. While punk rock rushed over the old world, Alex, Geddy and Neil would be trying to break a sound that the pundits said was dead. But there were several factors playing in their favour. Just because The Sex Pistols and The Damned were rocketing up the charts did not mean that there was not an audience for hard and progressive rock. The band also had a feisty champion in Geoff Barton of *Sounds* Magazine, later to become editor of *Kerrang!* Barton heard an import copy of 'All The World's A Stage' and was blown away. He raved about the record, calling Rush the best undiscovered band in Britain. This stirred interest in the group and by the time they hit England, they found themselves something of a cult phenomenon.

The band opened in Sheffield on June 1, and Alex, Geddy and Neil were surprised to find they had sold out the gig. All other dates on the jaunt were also SRO.

With the brief series of European dates more successful than the group expected, it was time to head into the studio. The band were originally going to record in London, but they ended up laying down most of the tracks at Rockfield Studios in South Wales.

Since Canada and the United States had very similar cultures, travelling in the US did not seem that different to the band and crew. But the European tour brought most of the entourage in contact with foreign cultures for the very first time. They quickly grew homesick and the band would always remember this when comparing their marathon swings across the US with tours by English acts.

Liam talked about how it felt to be away from home. 'The tour seemed very long, and then we went right into the wilds of Wales, into the studio for a fairly long album. After you're away from home for so long, you have a craving to get back. The studio was extremely isolated. There was a town a few miles down the road, but it was a very small, very old place. We were definitely out in the wilds. It was a very rustic setting. On the other hand it was a nice experience going into a different studio, but it wasn't the lap of luxury by any stretch of the imagination.'

One familiar face was perfectly comfortable with the setting. Terry was back in his native land producing his favourite band.

When the trio entered Rockfield studios much of the album was already written. It even had a working title, 'Closer To The Heart'. During the course of the sessions, 'A Farewell To Kings', 'Madrigal', and 'Cinderella Man' were written in their entirety. Work was also completed on 'Cygnus X-1'. To get the unique sound they wanted for the futuristic space epic, 'We allocated a day for creating some special environments,' according to Terry, 'which you can't just pull out of a hat.' So we messed around and had Alex hook up his guitar through various pedals and we hooked up a bunch of digital units in the control room. We just developed ideas with tape loops, a whole bunch of different sounds.'

Reading as always was having a profound effect on Neil's writing. He had been inspired to write 'Cygnus X-1' by an article on black holes in *Time* magazine. The genesis of another song came for the first time from an outsider. A friend of Neil's, Peter Talbot, gave the band the title 'Closer To The Heart' and the first verse 'And the men who hold high places, must be the ones who start to mould a new reality, closer to the heart.'

After spending three weeks at Rockfield, Terry and the band went to Advision Studios in London for

In Stockholm.

Europe at last – drive 'til you die.

Rush with Terry Brown.

sound and identity as a band. It is passionate, yet with a strong intelligence. The words convey the theme in a clear manner and the music supports the lyrics, and both work off each other. The louder, more aggressive passages are not just there so the group can rock out, they serve the story. The same is true of the quieter parts. If in the past they sometimes seemed merely a place to show that Rush were not just a heavy metal band, now they also serve the ideas the trio were trying to convey.

The second side also begins on a quiet note. 'Closer To The Heart' appears to be a manifesto of how the group would like things to be. Often accused of a coldly intellectual approach, they urge compassion and understanding. It remains a favourite with female Rush fans and would open quite a few radio station doors. Next comes 'Cinderella Man', a fable with lyrics from Geddy, and a beautiful melodic chorus. The band is able to soften its approach here without losing any of its intensity.

On any previous Rush album the next song would be a kick-out-the-jams rocker, but with 'Madrigal' the band spins another enchanting melody and does an all-out love song. The tune opens with two bittersweet lines from Neil, 'When the dragons grow too mighty, to slay with pen or sword.' Geddy's voice convincingly carries a tone of weariness that the whole band must have felt. They had had very little time off since the summer and they were far away from home. Neil's pen is way north-west of Pegasus on the album closer 'Cygnus X-1 Book One'. It builds on the developments of 'Caress Of Steel' and '2112'. But the group is better able to carry out its ambitions. As a reminder of the past a heavily synthesized voice sets up the saga that is to follow.

We learn of a black hole and its dangers and mysteries. The sharpest playing of the record follows as the menace is conveyed through a staccato instrumental passage. The percussion work seems enough to frighten off all but the most hardy character. But the traveller heads onwards in his ship, the 'Rocinante' towards the heart of the dead star. But what awaits him is not known, but it is clearly worth the risk. The ship enters the black hole 'spinning, whirling still descending like a spiral sea unending.' A brief phrase 'to be continued' closes out the lyrics, and leaves listeners wondering if they will ever hear the fate of the 'Rocinante'. Incidentally, 'Rocinante' is the name of Steinbeck's motor home in his book 'Travels With Charlie'. It was also the name of Don Quixote's horse.

After completing 'Kings' the group moved to Canada to work on their first video. Alex, Geddy and

two weeks of mixing. Again, the band had made a leap forward.

The album opens on a meditative note as Alex plays a short classical guitar introduction. Birds at Rockfield can be heard whistling in the background as Neil joins in with chimes, triangle and other percussion. Geddy also plays a meditative synthesizer pattern. The band then pause for a moment before the traditional power attack. As Geddy wonders what future generations will think of us, the band plays with anger.

The subject turns to the problems of today. Then comes an instrumental break that shows the band as hard-hitting as ever, but a little leaner and with a more focused idea of where they are going. It is the same trio as before, yet different. The metallic rock of the earlier albums remains, but the arrangements and the sound are fuller. Geddy puts in a great performance. He seems to be angry that the 'hypocrites are slandering the sacred halls of truth.'

The remainder of side one finds the band in search of 'Xanadu'. The desperate quest is successful in ways beyond the narrator's imagination and, to his horror, he finds what he is looking for. Instrumentally there is the same stretching that appears on 'A Farewell To Kings'. They have absorbed the progressive rock influences they sought, but even more than on '2112' they have created their own

Neil were filmed playing in a mock concert at Toronto's Seneca College. 'A Farewell To Kings', 'Xanadu' and 'Closer To The Heart' were shot. Pictures of rural English castles decorated the acoustic opening to the title song.

The buildings in the background on the cover to 'A Farewell To Kings' are in Toronto. For years Rush fans have tried to figure out where in the city the picture was taken from. The foreground of the cover is a separate photograph shot at a demolished warehouse in Buffalo, New York. That picture was matted with a photo of the Toronto skyline. One of those most perplexed about the cover is none other than Rush's road manager Howard Ungerleider who lives in one of those buildings!

The band had been working for almost 10 solid months. They would now have one month off before it was time to start gearing up for what would become known as 'The Drive 'Til You Die Tour'.

For even with the time off, the group and the crew were still not totally recovered from the marathon tour they had so recently completed. But with radio still a problem and a reputation as a live band to live up to, they would have to hit the road again in September

when the new album was released. Rush played just about every town in which they could get a date. A few weeks might see them play 15 or more dates in six or seven cities all across America. And this was not even including Canada or the now obligatory European tour, and there was now the possibility of going to other parts of the world. Both Geddy and Alex were later to say that all the tours from '2112' through to 'Hemispheres' seemed like one unending string of dates.

But life as a road band was continuing to increase the band's prospects. When 'A Farewell To Kings' came out in September in Great Britain, the United States and Canada, it was the first time a Rush album had been released simultaneously in all three countries.

The strongest sign that Rush had finally arrived came two months later. On the US leg of the tour, the group found itself headlining in most cities, although they still played a few shows as special guests. In November three Rush records were certified gold in the United States on the same day. 'A Farewell To Kings' led the list, followed by 'All The World's A Stage' and '2112'. While sales of 50,000 records would garner a Canadian Gold album (because Canada has a much smaller population), sales of half a million copies of a recording are needed to receive the American version of the award. After playing across the continent for four years the band's commitment and integrity had paid off.

It was at the end of that month that they returned to Philadelphia where I got a chance to see what was now my favourite band for the second time.

Rush made their second appearance at the Tower Theatre on November 26. Like their first show it was sold out. As the crowd lined up outside the venue, the mood was electric, and it was clear that Rush would be playing a bigger hall on their next tour, and this was the last chance to see them in a more intimate setting.

Tom Petty And The Heartbreakers played for 30 uninspiring minutes. When they left the stage, the crowd began screaming 'Rush, Rush, Rush!' But Tom and the boys came back for an encore. It was hard to hear their heartless rendition of 'Breakdown' over the cries for Alex, Geddy and Neil. There was a brief intermission, then the show began.

The whole stage turned black for a moment. Then Terry Brown's strange voice intoned, 'In the constellation of Cygnus there lurks a mysterious, invisible force. The black hole of Cygnus X-1." After the Rocinante's final flash of glory, Geddy's Rick travels onward towards the six stars of the Northern Cross. He is joined by Neil, and eventually Alex as live Rush increases the drama of the studio version tenfold.

Other favourites were performed with that unique Rush mix of grace and abandon, '2112', 'Cinderella Man', 'A Farewell To Kings', 'By-Tor And The Snowdog', and 'Lakeside Park'.

When I heard 'A Farewell To Kings' I knew the band were shooting for new musical territory and, seeing them live, I became fully convinced they had commanded this newly charted course.

It was also interesting to see how the new musical direction had influenced their stage set-up. Neil was sporting his new jet black Slingerlands complete with the star in a circle logo on his bass drums. He had even more percussion instruments than ever before. Alex was in a transitional period with his amps. He had Hi-Watt heads, and Marshall cabinets. Geddy had a combination double neck guitar-bass, the first one ever produced by Rickenbacker who made it specially for Geddy. In addition, he used a Mini-Moog during a few of the songs and was also playing bass pedals.

The trio later said that even though they were able to play the new material live, they learned a valuable lesson from the 'Kings' tour. With all the

added equipment, they had made things very difficult for themselves by not figuring out how to play all of the new songs on stage before the tour rehearsals. Geddy found he would be playing an irregular rhythm with his feet, and playing the melody with his hands and singing on top of that. With the increased musical complexity, the band's stage manner was a little toned down. Since they were so busy playing, they were not able to run around as much as they had in the past. Some of that excitement was now expressed in purely musical terms.

The actual stage production had also grown. The PA speakers literally reached to the ceiling of the hall. Aircraft landing lights lit up the venue during key songs. It was the most gear I had ever seen stuffed into the 3,500 seat theatre.

My phone calls to local radio stations increased after the performance. I also found that more and more people had actually heard of the band. My missionary efforts increased.

On Christmas Day I received an unexpected present. A friend called to tell me that Rush were on television. I ran to the set and turned it on, cranking up the volume. For some reason Don Kirschner's rock concert was on at 2pm in the afternoon. I saw the band rip through the three 'Farewell To Kings' videos. It was my favourite present that year.

After a short holiday break the band were on the road again in North America, and in February they embarked on their second British tour on which all 16 dates were sold out. Rush found that just like in the East Coast region of the United States their audience was growing, but these foreign gigs were not without controversy when *NME* writer, Miles, launched a personal attack against Neil Peart and the band. The article all but branded Rush a band of Nazi fascists. Geddy witnessed the conversation between Neil and Miles and couldn't believe how the interview was taken completely out of context.

It was a very painful couple of weeks for Geddy. His parents had survived a Nazi concentration camp during the war, and his father actually died from its effects after moving to Canada to start a new life for his family.

Things quietened down a bit as the band left Europe, but it was time for more shows in the United States. They continued playing, sometimes up to 13 days in a row in 13 different cities. Their popularity also spurred Mercury to make an unusual marketing move. Rush's appeal came not from a radical change in direction, but a natural progression. Mercury also saw a growth in the sales of their earlier albums. With a new record not due out until autumn, the company

decided to take advantage of the growing interest in the band by releasing their first three albums as a specially priced three album set. It was dubbed 'Archives' and helped give some of the group's later fans a sense of the trio's recording history. Neil was particularly pleased because the package contained the third album. 'There is some great music in 'Caress Of Steel', he said at the time, 'and with 'Archives' more people will get a chance to hear that music."

Rush continued their gruelling series of gigs into June when they closed out the 'Drive 'Til You Die' tour with a few more Canadian shows. They had played in front of more than one million people. Alex, Geddy and Neil had also received their second Juno award, this time for best group of the year. At this point they had six gold and three platinum records in their homeland.

But a prolonged rest was not on the cards for the three very exhausted musicians. First there was the little matter of a new album to record. And the growing amounts of headline dates left them with less of a chance to write on the road. For the first time they would do almost all of the writing in the studio. Once again, Terry would co-produce. A return trip to Rockfield was set up.

We almost died by the end of the 'Kings' tour," recalls Alex. "That was the tour where we'd work for 12 days, have a day off, work for nine days; have a day off. We got really burned out! It was a very tough tour. We worked a lot that year. We had a week off, then we went to England and started writing 'Hemispheres'. We were in a rehearsal house about a mile from Rockfield for two weeks. We'd finish writing and rehearsing one morning at 10 o'clock. The crew came in at noon, moved the gear to the studio where we were working by four that afternoon. The material wasn't all written, we were still stuck on a few things so we ploughed through. Once we started working we figured we're OK, we're gonna finish.

"We had planned five days off at the end of the recording session before mixing in London, maybe go to Europe for a few days and just relax. And we went overtime. We were there at Rockfield until two in the morning the day that the other band were coming in. We managed to push them off for a few days. They weren't really in a hurry. Thank goodness that they would do that. We were late on everything. We had one evening off, when we recorded the album. We worked for about five weeks straight on the recording end of it. We left for London that morning. Two o'clock in the morning. Went into the studio at noon that day at Advision, started mixing; we were there about 10 days. Nothing was working. It sounded awful. Everything sounded terrible. Gedd had some vocals that he had to do, that he did at Advision. It was a very trying time for him. It wasn't working out for him . . . very, very tense. To go through that at the end of the tour. We were in England for three months throughout 'Hemispheres'.

"At that point, while in Advision, Broon was almost out of his mind and Terry never gets angry and he was. I've never seen him like that before or since. And he said 'I have to get out of here'. He took the tapes around to three or four studios, just to hear them in another studio and he finally went into Trident, put them on and found the problem.

At Rockfield Studios in Wales.

He heard everything that was wrong with the mixes at that point, that he couldn't pin down before. We'd had a lot of really good fortune with 'A Farewell To Kings' at Advision. 'Hemispheres' had a different feel to it, and it was just not happening. At Trident everything stood out. We moved all the tapes there. Managed to book two weeks and mixed 'Hemispheres' there.

"By the end of it we were happy to go. We had two parties! A private party on the second to last night and we had just us and Terry, and the guys that worked at the studio. We got totally out of it! We had a very, very good time that night. The following night we had some friends over, and we had some champagne. It was such a relief to get over that whole thing, and to get home. We couldn't wait to get home.

Alex's bad dream — into the hemisphere.

The entire year was really hard. At the time we were all quite happy with the record. We felt that all the blood, sweat and tears had been worth it. It was another album that was a transitional album for us. 'Hemispheres' was an important album for us to do.

"'Hemispheres' set us up really well for what was to come next. When I listen to that album now, it's a dark album for me to listen to. I suppose I associate the whole tenseness and frustration and really hard work that went into that."

Geddy later explained why he thought they had run into problems during the recording of the album. "With every album, we want it to be that much more perfect. (With 'Hemispheres') the material changed and the approach to recording the material had to change to a certain degree because the music called for a different tone."

One of the songs that required a new approach was 'La Villa Strangiato (Weird City)'. "It was sort of a heavy release for us," said Geddy. "There were a lot of different ideas about music we wanted to put into a song. We wanted to put together a very complex song that had a lot of different time changes and had a lot of really radical changes in mood and rhythm. A little bit of humour is in there also. We spent more time recording 'Strangiato' than the entire 'Fly By Night' album. It's recorded in one take.

But it took 40 takes to get it right! It was our first piece without any vocals at all. So each section had to stand up with a theme and musical structure of its own."

And 'Strangiato' was not the most ambitious composition on the record. That distinction was reserved for 'Cygnus X-1 Book II - Hemispheres'.

"The basic idea came from a book I was reading called 'Powers Of Mind'," says Neil, "and it was just an incidental thing that was mentioned in the book, but it was something I'd read before so I tied it into a whole lot of things and it's the basic constant conflict between thoughts and emotions, between your feelings and your sort of rational ideas. Apollo and Dionysius have been used in a lot of books to sort of characterise those two elements, the rational side and the instinctive side. I've always been really interested in the way that those two themes transmit themselves into people in political life or in social life. All those conflicts are always going on between people. Whether the instinctive way is right or the rationally thought out way is right, and the basic theme of 'Hemispheres' is that conflict, the battle of the heart and mind.

"'Armageddon' is really the focus of that. It's the climax of that conflict and our hero Cygnus comes in and breaks up the conflict between Apollo and Dionysius. One of the main points that I wanted to make in the lyrics is that the battle is inside each of us. It's not some abstract cosmic battle, it's part of our everyday personal lives. So much of what we do in a day is governed by an idea or a feeling, and sometimes they can be battling each other."

That idea and others comes through loud and clear on the side-long epic. It achieves a unity that such longer pieces on 'Caress Of Steel' and '2112' were unable to attain. While the other long compositions seemed like stitched together song cycles, 'Hemispheres' is a complete piece of music. Evidence of the thematic and musical unity can even be found in the special effects: during the 'Armageddon' section as Geddy sings the word 'hemispheres' the left and right channels of the recording phase back and forth, emphasising the conflict between the two hemispheres of the brain.

Musically the familiar Rush sound undergoes further refinement. Even more than on the previous record, the music serves the lyrics and vice versa. The additional instruments are even more integrated into the piece.

Neil's lyrics continue to grow. They are as full of drama as ever, but they take on a more balanced and tolerant tone. The symbolic characters do not represent good and evil, but different points of view that must be reconciled.

Side two opens with a much shorter song, 'Circumstances', an interesting combination of the personal and the universal. The first two verses appear to refer to Neil's frustrating first trip to England. The chorus talks about the experience in more general terms as it discusses the chances we all take, the circumstances they occur in, and the way that the more things change, the more they seem to stay the same. The French phrase in the chorus besides conveying the latter thought more concisely also shows Neil's growing interest in the language. A few years later the three members of Rush began studying French. Neil himself had spent time in the French speaking Province of Quebec, and this motivated him to learn the language. The final two verses recall what appears to be Neil's personal experiences, as the song's character reflects on his current position and realises that all the things he once dreamed of as 'a boy alone and so far from home' have become reality. But the character still feels that he is the same person he was then. The song also contains a strong melody and even stronger playing from the trio.

'Circumstances' is followed by a squabble between the maples and the oak with tragi-comic results. In the 'Trees' the maples think that the oaks have far too much light. So the maples organise and move to cast off the oak tyranny. Unfortunately the result is that the trees are all made equal by 'hatchet . . . axe and saw.'

The album's closer is 'La Villa Strangiato' sub titled 'An Exercise In Self-Indulgence'. The weird city features the most intense playing on the record. What appears to be a studio production was actually performed live in one take. While on earlier recording the band seemed to be trying to imitate the musical prowess of their idols, here they are actually outplaying many of them. The compositional foundation for the song is taken from weird dreams that Alex often had. Each of the separate musical themes is based on individual dreams.

With the album taking much longer than expected to complete, Rush found that they had only a few weeks off as they made some videos and prepared for another round of touring. The album was scheduled for release in October; the gigs also started that month.

Despite the fact that it was Super Bowl Sunday, the biggest day of the year for American sports fans, more than 14,000 fans surfaced for Rush's concert at the Philadelphia Spectrum on January 21. Blondie, the opening act, was a bad choice by the promoter because they were thrown off the stage in less than 20 minutes. These fans were hard-core! They had come to see Rush, so when Blondie's guitar player gave Philly his middle finger, the stage became filled with debris and on came the PA.

The crowd was fired up after booing Blondie, and it seemed to make us rant for Rush all the more. It was a general admission show and the floor became a flowing river of Rush fans following each and every note unleashed by Lee and Lifeson. Peart's percussive pounding left future Philadelphia drummers pondering their fate.

Hands were held high above the crowd on Lee's lyrical passage 'we only stop for the best' complete with black Rickenbacker double neck. A new dimension was added on 'Cygnus X-I Book One The Voyage' and 'Book II Hemispheres'. Scriptures on the rear-projection screen pronounce the Prologue. The constellation of Cygnus is in sight with the six stars of the Northern Cross. Through the astral door the Rocinante is seen spinning timelessly through the spiralled space. At the end of 28-plus minutes of continuous music left and right hemispheres are united and we see the single perfect sphere.

Rush's grand finale was a presentation of the entire overture to '2112' (minus the Dream!). In the end Philly fans spilled over onto the floor, obviously in the mood for more. Rush responded with a medley of early classics including 'Working Man' and 'Bastille Day'.

Around this time the group won its second Juno award for best group of the year. But Alex, Geddy and Neil felt the weight of their growing popularity. "We were very, very careful not to let it get the best of us," says Alex. "That sudden success could really change you. You become lazy and constantly have other people doing things for you, and you lose perspective on why you're there and what you're doing."

For Neil . . . "The success put a strain on the friendship and it put a strain on the day-to-day relationships. It is something that we did go through at the time, we were not immune to it, but we were able to overcome the strain just by our closeness. We were able to help each other with difficulties like that and learned to deal with the pressure of things."

Geddy agrees with the other two's observations about the period. They could now indulge in, and be able to pay for, just about anything they wanted, a situation that had led to other bands growing apart in the past.

A six-week European jaunt began in mid-May at

the Newcastle City Hall in the UK. Five of the 18 dates were in London where demand for tickets increased dramatically after the 'Farewell To Kings' tour. Next came Belgium, West Germany, Sweden, Denmark, Norway and Switzerland. The eight-month tour ended June 4 in Geleen, Holland, at an outdoor rock festival with Mick Jagger, Peter Tosh, The Police and Dire Straits. The event was dubbed the Pink Pop Festival.

By this time touring was no longer a financial necessity for the band, but according to Neil it was a "musical necessity. Not only do we develop so much as individual musicians . . . it is valuable to our development as a unit. The observations that I make on the road looking at people and cities and watching the little trips going on between people and their emotional relationships, I love observing it all. I am a constant observer."

The band then took the summer off to write new material. Work was pretty much completed on three new songs, 'Jacob's Ladder', 'The Spirit Of Radio', and 'Freewill'. Even this working vacation was a relief to the trio who now had six weeks off the road - their longest break in five years.

It was soon over as the band embarked on a comparatively short four-week tour to break in the new material before recording. A show in Davenport, Iowa, on August 17 started things off, and included in the itinerary was a concert at Varsity Stadium in Toronto on September 2.

By the time this concert began the place was only about half-filled - quite a surprise. Local fans said many of their friends had seen the band half a dozen times or more and were going to skip the show. It seemed a rather unfriendly welcome home.

Another Toronto group, FM, opened the show and I realised that there was a distinct disadvantage to our seats. The 12-foot high stage made it impossible to see the musicians playing if you were sitting down, but I figured out that once Rush started playing, everyone would stand up and we would have the best seats in the house.

I was proved right, at least at first. When the intro music to '2112' came on, the crowd rose to its feet. Geddy began going wild ripping improvised riffs on his black Rickenbacker as he wailed through 'Overture' and 'The Temples Of Syrinx'. It turned out to be the best version of the song I ever heard. Unfortunately much of the audience did not deserve such a spirited performance. About halfway through the song, fans in the back of the field began screaming for those in the front to sit down. Then someone got the bright idea that grabbing handfuls of sod and throwing it at the

On the tour coach.

people up front would be a good form of crowd control. Within a minute or two several hundred people joined in.

Things got so ridiculous that we finally left the front and went towards the rear of the stadium and did our best Canadian audience imitation. When the trio introduced 'The Spirit of Radio' there was almost no applause before or after the song. The show was quite a disappointment. The audience seemed blasé throughout, even when the band were playing in top form. As the concert progressed you could tell Alex, Geddy and Neil were discouraged.

Ten days later, on the last North American date of the tour in Allentown, Pennsylvania, it was a completely different story. It was an outdoor show at the Allentown Fairgrounds. Oddly enough there was even a handful of Toronto fans down for the show and they agreed that the Varsity Stadium gig had been a real letdown. At the height of his popularity, Pat Travers opened this show and the rowdy capacity crowd of 25,000 gave him a strong reception.

Rush again kicked off the set with '2112', and the difference in the atmosphere was immediately apparent. It seemed like everyone in the place was pushing to get up front. The crush of people near the barrier was incredible, and at one point it actually broke, creating a dangerous situation. The audience surged back and forth and came close to being smacked into the wooden beams and nails jutting out from the wreckage. Geddy was able to calm things down long enough for it to be pieced back together.

The group played a great set, but this night was different. The combination of their playing and the emotional feedback from the audience made the show one of those standout gigs among hundreds. Rush were right on, throughout, more certain of the new songs and freer on the old ones.

The band's sense of fun was also in evidence. Pat Travers joined in, and Rush became a four-piece for a raunchy version of 'Working Man'. Geddy announced it was the last night of the North American tour as the road crew carried the band's pilot, ducktaped like a Mummy, onto the stage. Alex played an all-out heavy metal solo while sitting on top of the hapless flyboy.

The pilot was in Allentown to fly the band back by night to Toronto so they could spend a few days with their families, but within 11 days they were back in England to play their last two live dates of the 1970s, a pair of shows at Stafford Bingley Hall. Attendance passed the 20,000 mark and fans were turned away at both concerts.

After the English encore dates it was back to Canada to work on influencing the music of the 80's.

CHAPTER 8

With the tour over it was time to actually start recording the new album. Rough demos of several songs had already been laid down, and the extended vacation and warm-up shows gave Rush extra time to work on the new material. The recording itself would be done closer to home at Quebec's Le Studio. Alex, Geddy, Neil and Terry met at the facility in late September, and stayed there through much of the next month.

All concerned were going after a different sound and approach. 'Hemispheres' had reached the outer limits of seventies art rock with its extended composition, complex musical structures, and in-depth treatment of metaphysical ideas. It seemed that they had explored to their fullest a whole range of topics. But now Rush wanted to chart a new course for a new decade.

While the band had often been unfavourably compared by many critics to new wave and punk groups, the trio had listened to the new sounds, and if all of it was not their musical cup of tea, they of all groups understood that constant change was crucial to rock.

Alex, Geddy and Neil were particularly interested by the music of Ultravox, Japan and Peter Gabriel who were infusing the new wave spirit with heavy doses of electronics and rhythm. Rush saw how these new directions were similar to the ideas they had explored on the 'Cygnus' epic.

Preparing to meet a new decade on their own terms was not always easy for the group. Some ideas would have to be jettisoned. Neil had been working on another long story. It was based on the ancient Arthurian legend of 'Sir Gawain And The Green Knight'. One rendering in verse is one of the oldest pieces of English literature around. Its author is unknown. Most of the other new material had a more modern sensibility, and after much consideration Neil realised that the concept would seem out of place in the band's current gameplan. It was dropped.

Neil went to his writing cottage in Quebec and began working on something to replace the piece. From Peart's pen emerged an artistic expression of

Painting permanent pictures.

musical integrity titled 'Natural Science'. It would eventually clock in at over nine minutes, and was constructed differently from its predecessors. Gone were the symbolic characters of earlier extended Rush songs. Neil was talking directly to the audience. The song reflects several different themes. As always the concept of balance is important to him. His devotion to the middle ground is intense. If Neil is fanatical about anything, it is the concept of balance. 'Natural Science' is interesting because the lyrics make connections that do not always leap forward towards us. Interrelationships between music, nature, and science are illustrated.

Neil Peart talked with Jim Ladd about some of the concerns that guided him during the writing of the lyrics. "I think there are a lot of great strides being taken by man," said Neil. "It's also true of art. For all of the corruption that goes on, there are lots of worthwhile things also. You can look at the cinema, books being written, newspapers . . . you can look at any manifestation of our existence here, and you can see a positive and a negative side to it.

"I think that the scientific and mechanical world getting out of hand is a symptom, but it is also a symptom of that positive quest to know. That drive which I think is one of the most precious things we have, if it is contained within a reasonable focus.

"Obviously the original relationship between man and nature was that he had to tame it in order to survive, and that became more and more sophisticated and out of hand, and finally it just became destruction. It's become the same thing with science where people don't understand it, and they are afraid of it. They think that you have to eradicate science in order to control it. I think it needs a lot more awareness in people's minds about what science is, and what it is doing and why. In fact science is not some impersonal thing trying to destroy us. It's not an enemy, it's something we ourselves created, and if it gets out of hand, it is our fault for letting it get out of hand.

"So what it boils down to is that we have to take ourselves in hand more than anything. It is we that need the taming."

And that could refer not just to science, but to the music the band were trying to create. Rather than ignoring the changes in music or throwing out the sound they had worked on for years Rush were trying to incorporate what was valuable to them from all genres and times. They did not want to be part of the old wave, or the new. They wanted to continue to bury the world with a timeless flow of music. But taking the long view did not mean that they would become musical conservatives.

An example of this can be seen in their playing styles. Alex, Geddy and Neil had long since proved that they had the chops to run rings around most of the musicians in the business. Now they were working to refine their approaches. They realised that the ability to perform precisely difficult arrangements and patterns was not enough. So they spent more time than ever before on the composition of songs. Rush wanted to achieve an equilibrium between their influences, inspiration, technique and passion. Whether or not they would be able to succeed, would show whether Rush would be able to continue as a viable musical force in the 1980's.

This conscious charting of a future course could be seen in the way the album was prepared. Some of the material was worked out at leisure and then road tested in front of a live audience. 'Natural Science' came together in a bout of creative tension with time constraints weighing heavily on the trio. In contrast, 'Different Strings' was designed as a purely studio creation to test the band's most ornate musical instincts. On 'Different Strings' Hugh Syme made another guest appearance. This time he played Le Studio's grand piano.

release. One was the use of the famous 'Dewey Defeats Truman' headline from *The Chicago Tribune*.

Back in 1948 the paper jumped the gun and declared Dewey the winner in the race for the US Presidency. Truman managed to pull off a last-minute victory, and *The Tribune* was left with a considerable amount of yoke on its pages. While this had occurred several decades previously, the paper was still sensitive about the incident and refused to permit its use. So the headline had to be whited out. A Coca-Cola sign was also visible, but the folks at Coke objected to the sign's proximity to the smiling woman's semi-naked thighs. This was replaced by commercial signs carrying the three band members' names. The Pearl beer sign became Peart.

Since Geddy was off producing an album by the group Wireless and Alex was on vacation, Neil found that he had to deal with the fallout over the cover. He recalled constantly getting phone calls from the record company saying they could not do this or that. However, the problems were eventually washed away.

'Permanent Waves' was finally released on January 1, 1980. It was the first record released in the new decade, and it set a new standard in sound, playing, and composition for the 1980s.

'The Spirit Of Radio', the lead-off track, demonstrates the band's new sound with its upbeat melody and strong rhythmic base. Lyrically the song is both hopeful and pessimistic, describing an ideal radio station that really exists and comparing it with the commercialised stations that play it safe in the interest of profits. It also indirectly salutes an old friend, David Marsden, programme director at Toronto's CFNY, the man who first played Rush on the radio.

The station still flies high the flag of free form radio. 'The Spirit Of Radio' praises this approach and castigates stations that have abandoned it. Oddly enough this attack would unlock the doors to radio airplay for Rush.

For Marsden . . . "It was really flattering that they wrote the song about the station. We don't even play that much Rush, but they were obviously quite taken with our willingness to play bands before anyone else would go near them."

'Freewill' continues the strong bright approach of 'The Spirit Of Radio'. The sound is crisp and clean as Geddy sings Neil's words about choices we must all make even if we deny that choices exist. 'Jacob's Ladder' uses Biblical imagery to describe the search for inspiration. Alex's guitar style comes into its own on this album and especially on this song, fusing

Once the basic tracks were completed, Rush headed to England to do the final mixes at Trident Studios. Trident was the place where they broke the mixing log-jam that developed on 'Hemispheres' and it once again helped the flow of 'Permanent Waves'.

Geddy reflected on how the group's approach had changed. "I think the important lesson that we learned over the past few years is that music should be a natural thing. That it shouldn't be forced. Fortunately the more successful you become, the more you get to practise that kind of philosophy. We don't really want to guess where we are going. We just want to get together at certain intervals, and see what we start writing, so it's more of an honest, natural approach."

This approach would pay off, but first there were a few problems that had to be taken care of. They stemmed from Hugh's clever ideas about how to design the cover. The working title of the album was 'Wavelength'. Originally Hugh was going for a high tech look by using E-K-G images of the band's heartbeats, but then he got an even wilder idea. He would show a smiling woman standing in front of a wave sweeping through a shore town. Several elements of the image had to be removed for the US

elements of classical, jazz-rock, heavy metal, progressive rock and reggae.

'Entre Nous' or 'Between Us' is another fusing of the personal and the universal. At one level it is a conversation between two lovers, but it also addresses the connections and separations between the trio and their audience. There is a frank message from the group to their fans in, 'Just between us, I think it's time for us to realise, the spaces in between, leave room for you and I to grow.'

The studio production 'Different Strings' allows the band to stretch out. Geddy talked about his approach to the song during an interview printed in *Guitar Player* magazine. "There's one song on the new album called 'Different Strings' in which harmonics become quite an integral part of the piece," he said. "The bass part is very simple - a punctuating sort of rhythm - but in between the notes I popped a couple of harmonics on two (different) strings at the fifth fret."

Another interesting aspect of the song is its lyrical concerns. Geddy wrote the words, but if you did not know this you would think Neil had, since the song shares many of the same thematic concerns of the rest of the album, lost innocence, the differences between people and the difficulty of communication. This raises an important point about Rush. Many of the topics they address in their songs are not just exclusive concerns of any one band member. All three of them share in many ways a common viewpoint about music, society, values and how they want to conduct themselves. That's why it's not quite right to talk about many of their ideas as being Geddy's or Neil's or Alex's. When three people work as closely as they do, an incredible exchange of attitudes takes place.

'Natural Science' closes the record, and for Rush fans it is perhaps the best nine minutes and 26 seconds ever put on to vinyl. The song is complex in just about every way, with an amazing fusion of different styles and time changes - everything from acoustic rock, to progressive music prowess, to the Rush power surge, to the latest in electronic experimentation. Lyrically there are several different themes and ideas intertwined to make a coherent whole.

'Permanent Waves' as a whole is a giant step forward for Rush. A new maturity and control emerges on the album and it would win the band respect in many quarters where before they had been ridiculed. Even the most difficult and complex segments are presented in such a way as to make the album easily accessible. The band had figured out

how to express themselves in a way that would be pleasing to fans of many different types of music without compromising their own standards. A word of praise should be reserved also for Terry Brown. On this recording he really came into his own. The sound quality is superb. 'Permanent Waves' sounds as fresh today as the day it was completed, an achievement for all concerned. The last sound on the record is the moving of waves in and out on the sand which expresses what the band were seeking throughout the entire recording.

With the release of the album, The Permanent Waves Tour washed across America. This time Rush travelled with more than $600,000 worth of equipment. Four tractor trailers carted it all around and a crew of 25 people under Howard's direction were employed to keep things running smoothly. To transport the crew and band, two buses and a camper were used.

An early January gig in Binghamton, New York, at the Broome County Arena saw the band playing a rough, festive set. Coming off their longest break from touring in many years, they were still ironing the bugs out of the new set and equipment, but it was clear that the trio were glad to be back on stage. Alex seemed especially fired-up. During 'Xanadu' he played the bottom half of Geddy's double neck, while Geddy played the top half. As they made that modern music the audience responded with a crackle of bright emotional feedback. Two highlights of the show were strong readings of 'Jacob's Ladder' and 'Natural Science'.

While the vast majority of the gigs featured this same interplay between the band and its audience, there was a reminder of what could happen early in the tour. When tickets went on sale for a Detroit gig on January 12, about 1,200 fans got out of hand and smashed ticket booth doors and windows. Although no one was seriously injured, the police had to be called in to restore order.

As the tour progressed, the album began to appear on just about every radio playlist. Ironically, the song most heard was 'The Spirit Of Radio'. It even got airplay on Top 40 radio stations. With this magic music leading the way, the record began to take off. Album oriented stations were playing it in heavy rotation, and on *Billboard*'s album chart the disc peaked at number four where it managed to hold steady for several weeks. In England the album pushed up one more notch to number three. By March 'Permanent Waves' had gone Platinum in Canada, Gold in the States and Silver in England.

But there were drawbacks to their increasing

popularity. While in their early days they had been ignored by radio station personnel, record company types and assorted industry hangers-on, now they found more and more people who did not even know who they were, trying to meet them because of their chart position. It was very frustrating for the group. By remaining true to themselves, they had managed to attract the very people they did not want to deal with.

In a way they were more comfortable when the rock industry and press had been unanimously slagging them. They still had plenty of critics, however. At this time one Philadelphia disc jockey, who later helped to pioneer the use of music on television, said to me, "Rush have got to be the worst band in the world. I hate Rush. That singer should be shot for singing like that."

As the band's popularity continued to grow, I continued calling the local stations telling them to play more Rush. But what I was looking forward to most was their next Philadelphia appearance. Soon after I received news that they would not be playing in Philly. The reason, two of the town's sports teams were heading towards the play-offs, so the Spectrum was unavailable while the band would be in the north-eastern part of the US. I immediately called their management office, telling anyone who would listen that the band should come back later and play a gig since Philadelphia was their strongest city in the region. The staff were sympathetic, but they said the decision had been made. So the next thing I decided to do was to call my acquaintances at the local radio

station, which was playing Rush, and get a petition drive going. Soon after, the programme director Steve Sutton got in touch with me and said he liked the idea and asked me to come in and organise it. With the radio station pushing the petition, there was an immediate response and eventually over 16,000 signatures petitioned Rush to play in Philadelphia. Steve even sponsored my idea to have a 'Rush Bus Contest' where we had local fans write in postcards to win tickets and bus rides to a Rush concert in Hershey, Pennsylvania, two hours drive from Philadelphia.

With their increased success the band played multiple dates in most major cities. St. Louis fans saw the trio play three sold-out nights at Kiel Auditorium before more than 30,000. Rush played two nights in Milwaukee, Dallas, Seattle, Detroit and San Francisco. In the Los Angeles area four shows were performed and in Chicago they became the first act to sell-out the 12,000 seat International Amphitheatre for a four-night stand. But perhaps the biggest highlight of the tour would be an extended gig in New York City. Four nights at the Palladium would signal to the music industry that Rush had arrived.

Before these shows they received another boost, this time from English fans. In April the band and its individual members swept the readers' choice polls in both *Melody Maker* and *Sounds* magazines. They were cited for their talents as a group and their individual musicianship.

The Palladium shows were set for the week of May 9. My Junior Prom was May 10 and my girlfriend gave me the ultimatum, either her or Rush. The band were in top form for the concerts. They had been on the road for four months and the rough edges that were shown in Binghamton had been sanded down. Rush rocked their way through a great set including such songs as 'La Villa Strangiato', 'Jacob's Ladder', '2112', 'By-Tor And The Snowdog' and 'Xanadu'. The show was over two hours and many hard core fans were on hand. The audience followed every note knowing each twist and turn of even their most complex songs; air drummers were everywhere following Peart's percussive precision; hundreds of arms could be seen punching out the fills to the beginning of 'Xanadu'. Geddy once said he knew their audience contained many musicians and here was proof. Mouths dropped when later in the song it was time for the duelling double necks as Alex and Geddy wailed away at their Hydra-like guitars. The band did many of their longer pieces at these shows and with no opening act it was a special treat for Big Apple Rush fans.

It was at these shows that the band made an important decision about their next record. They had originally planned to record another live set, and several shows on the upcoming British leg of the tour were to be recorded. But at the Palladium shows, Uncle Cliff, who had left Mercury Records and branched out to management, told the band that they were crazy. He attended all the shows and after each one he told them that they were on a roll creatively and now was the time to go back into the studio. His constant badgering had an effect on Rush. By the week's end they came around to his point of view, even with the recording trucks already booked. A live album would have to wait. Instead of documenting just one tour, the record would capture their sound on two jaunts.

Incidentally, Cliff would make quite a name for himself as a manager. His frank opinions and no-nonsense approach would later serve him well in breaking in such bands as Def Leppard and Metallica.

But with all due credit going to Uncle Cliff, there were other factors that influenced the band. As Rush began headlining they started using their sound-checks to work on new musical ideas, and the results of these informal writing sessions were particularly fruitful on the Waves Tour.

Their last US date was another New York area appearance at the Nassau County Coliseum on Long Island, a wild, rowdy, sold out show where 17,000 Rush fans grooved to the music. During the encore that evening, Alex, Geddy and Neil returned to the stage wearing New York Islanders hockey jerseys. Geddy dedicated 'La Villa' to the Islanders who "are going to win the Stanley Cup tomorrow."

After the show I had my first opportunity to meet Geddy. The petition had received much publicity, and an interview was set up to discuss the possibility of a Philadelphia area appearance. I was nervous, and to make matters worse, this was the first interview I had ever done. Geddy could tell I was a big fan as I stood before him wearing a Rush tour shirt, trying not to drop my tape recorder. He was as relaxed as I was nervous, sitting on a couch drinking a glass of Chivas Regal as he said, "Don't worry Philly, we'll be playing at the Spectrum in September." Geddy also restated his prediction that the Islanders would beat the Philadelphia Flyers in the Stanley Cup play-offs. The game was set on a familiar date to 'Caress Of Steel' fans, May 24. Geddy was right.

The band then headed to Europe for another fully-fledged tour of the old continent. Gigs in Scotland and London were recorded for use on the live album. The reception from the British fans was intense and proof of their new-found celebrity came when the UK record company threw a big party for them to celebrate the end of the tour. With a five-month tour in the bag it was now time to head back home for some much needed rest and relaxation.

After a brief rest, the band decided to lend a helping hand to their friends and labelmates, Max Webster. In return, Pye Dubois, Webster's non-performing lyricist would give Rush the idea for one of their biggest songs to date. But more on that, just a few miles downstream.

While Alex, Geddy and Neil had never really liked jamming with other musicians, the members of Max Webster were an exception. They found that playing with Webster was an enjoyable, rewarding experience. Max's off the wall humour and solid musicianship complemented Rush's more controlled sound. Webster had opened quite a few dates on the Permanent Waves Tour and the bands played together in an informal setting at many a soundcheck. When Webster's Kim Mitchell suggested that the two groups get together in a recording studio for a battle of the bands everyone agreed. Appropriately the song (a favourite jamming number for Rush and Max Webster) was 'Battlescar'. "We set up both bands live," recalled Geddy, "and we had this producer Jack Richardson standing in the middle with a baton, sort of conducting us. We were all in a circle and he was in the middle, and we just recorded the tune."

Well actually not just recorded. Neil recalled that they had the song down after the third or fourth take, but everyone was enjoying themselves so much that they did it about 40 times.

The result is a delightful mix of two styles. Max Webster can be heard in the off the wall time changes. Rush are apparent in Geddy's screeching vocals. They recall some of his earliest work with the band but perhaps the best synthesis is achieved on the 'wall of drums' sound.

Their good turn to Max Webster paid off in spades when Pye Dubois gave Neil the basis for what eventually became 'Tom Sawyer'. Originally titled 'Louis The Warrior', the song's streetwise character was a different turn for the band and much appreciated.

Alex, Geddy and Neil then took a few weeks to go off by themselves and work on new material. 'The Camera Eye' was developed first, followed by 'Red Barchetta', 'Tom Sawyer', 'YYZ' and 'Limelight'. As August drew to a close, they paid a return visit to Phase One Studios to lay down demo tracks with Terry Brown. An initial stab at 'Witch Hunt' was also recorded. Left aside this time was a softer piece based on Thomas Hardy entitled 'Wessex Tales'. Much like 'Sir Gawain And The Green Knight', it did not sit comfortably with the direction in which the band was now moving.

That direction was an extension of 'Permanent Waves'. Rush were very comfortable with their efforts to meet the 1980s head on. They wanted to continue to streamline their approach and they were also fascinated by the renewed emphasis on rhythm in popular music as seen in the work of artists as diverse as Talking Heads, Third World and Bob Marley.

As was now a band tradition, some of the new material would be tested on a brief tour. A two-week sprint up the East Coast of the US would get Rush back into shape for 'Moving Pictures'. The first date was September 11, in Hampton, Virginia. As soon as I knew the itinerary, cheques were written and letters sent to coliseums from Virginia to Pennsylvania to Massachusetts.

The band were a little loose as they performed 'Tom Sawyer' and 'Limelight' for the very first time on a lighted stage. While 'Limelight' sounded much like its recorded verson, 'Tom Sawyer' was hopeful, yet discontent. Played in a faster tempo, it did not have the rhythmic punch of the completed version of the song.

The Coliseum should have been called Fort Hampton on September 11, because the security was so intense. "If you stand up one more time, I'm gonna throw you the fuck out of here," shouted the power-hungry guard from the front of the stage. I was the only person remotely getting into the music, so they must have thought I was a major security threat because 10 police officers then lined the front of the stage, which was low to the ground.

The rest of the audience sat in a stoned stupor as I argued with the cops who were now blocking my view of the band. "I didn't drive nine hours to look at your ugly face," I shouted during the acoustic opening of 'The Trees'. A minute later Alex stopped playing, came up to the front of the stage and yelled, "You guards get the fuck away from here! If he wants to stand, leave him alone!" All the security left the stage front as I rocked out for the rest of the night.

By the end of the tour 'Tom Sawyer' was much shorter in length. A lot of the jamming that had characterised the song in its Hampton performances was eliminated. The rhythmic drive was much clearer, although it still had an amphetamine-like tempo.

On September 25, Rush made their long awaited Philadelphia appearance. In a strange coincidence a member of Led Zeppelin, the band that had most

influenced Rush in their early years, died that day. John Bonham's pounding drum style had given Zeppelin the strong bottom that Page, Plant and Jones had built upon. The soaking wet crowd at the sold-out show were subdued. Rush played a weak set. Bruised and sullen storm clouds obscured the light of this day. Their performance was still tentative and lacked the fire they had at the Virginia concert.

After the show I met Alex and Neil for the first time. I was backstage to present all the petitions we had gathered asking for the band to play in Philadelphia. At the time it was a disheartening experience. Rush's growing success had forced them to adopt a kind of protective armour when dealing with record and radio industry types. As far as they were concerned at the time, that's exactly what I was. The worst moment came when Neil was looking at the petitions and spotted a bogus name. He called out, "Hey Geddy, look Janis Joplin wants us to play Philadelphia." Geddy and Alex tried to be as friendly as possible, but it was pretty obvious that their hearts were not in it. Although I was later to understand the pressures they were under and saw how they must have felt, it was an upsetting night for me. I had worked my ass off on the petition drive and it had been made a joke of. The band left the petitions behind as they moved on to another city.

I was so upset that I almost didn't make the trek to Springfield, Massachusetts. But on September 28, there I was in the front row, complete with a large box containing the petitions. Rush restored my faith as they put on a tremendous concert. Geddy threw me his pick, which I caught at the end of 'Xanadu'. During the encore I vented some frustration as the lighted stage became flooded with the Philadelphia petitions.

On September 30, in Allentown, before another great show, one of the Rush crew members told me that the band's tour bus had been broken into while in the City of Brotherly Love, Philly. Many personal items had been stolen.

The trio spent much of October and November in Le Studio recording 'Moving Pictures'. While the music was an extension of many of the ideas developed on 'Permanent Waves', the album had a darker thematic tone.

Paradoxically, their mass success had in a way upset the band. Technically it was another step forward. The band were in for the start of the digital age. 'Moving Pictures' was one of the first rock albums that was digitally mixed and mastered. As Alex said with "most of the music written, arranged, rehearsed and refined and all the rough edges smoothed out . . ." the initial process of laying down

the basic tracks was made much easier.

The inspiration for the songs came from their experiences of travel, dislocation and fame. Although there is much darkness on the album, there are several light spots, notably 'YYZ', pronounced Y-Y-Zed.

"We really had a strong idea to do a shorter, more concise instrumental that was actually a song with verses and a chorus, and so on, à la Weather Report," Neil says. The jazz-rock fusion influence had become increasingly important to the band's sound.

The title 'YYZ' refers to Toronto International Airport. It's the code that is used by the pilots and the control tower. The introduction to the song is actually the Morse code readout for 'YYZ'. "There are parts of that song," says Neil, "that are semi-evocative of the feelings that are engendered when you are going to the airport to leave. You are sort of feeling edgy and tense because you are having to leave home and go to work, and you are thinking that you are half at home and half away. It's a very transitional period, and you always have a sense of infinite possibilities at the airport. You can change your mind and fly anywhere in the world, and all of a sudden, you are not in Toronto any more, you are in the world. An airport really should not be said to be (in) a city, because it never is. It's always a crossroad. And that of course is a big part of the song. We tried to work a lot of the exotic nature of the airport in there. And the big sappy instrumental bridge in the middle that is really orchestrated, really emotional, really rich, is of course again half symbolising the tremendous emotional impact of coming home."

'Witch Hunt' was designed as the album's production number. Hugh Syme came in to play synthesizer again. This tune featured a strong melding of musical and lyrical themes. "When Alex and I first received those lyrics," said Geddy, "the scene was so vivid. I mean those lyrics are very cinematic; they are very visual. You read through it, and you have a clear-cut picture of the scene that is going on and we sat down and said 'okay, let's try to capture that imagery that the lyrics evoke.' We worked very carefully with that in mind . . . we looked at it very cinematically, which we've done in the past, but this time we did it totally."

Because 'Witch Hunt' had so captured their imagination, the band were especially painstaking in their recording of the tune. They re-worked it over and over again until they had it right. Eventually they were to play it live, even though they had never intended to perform it onstage beneath a flickering light.

The amount of work put into 'Witch Hunt' is best

illustrated in the introduction when a vigilante mob is heard being stirred up by a fanatic of one sort or another. It is purposely mixed so that you cannot understand what is being said, but the tenor of the situation, the hatred, the ill-will, and the fear comes through loud and clear. This effect was created by emptying the studio (in the middle of a snowy night) of production staff, road crew and band, and depositing everyone in the cold outside the isolated facility. With tape recorders rolling, Neil gave his best fanatic's speech, gradually getting more and more whipped up as everyone involved let themselves get carried away. The compact disc version of the recording brings this image into perspective with a stark clarity.

In sharp contrast to the work put into 'Witch Hunt', 'Red Barchetta' was put down in one take.

The new technology was most evident in the increased use of keyboards. Geddy found that his taking on another instrument was changing his musical approach. "When you get a new instrument, it's like starting all over again," he says. Geddy did more chordal work and on 'The Camera Eye' there was no electric bass on half the song. Instead the tune was carried by synths and drums. The band were working in the electro-pop and ska influences that Alex, Geddy and Neil were interested in. A similar approach was used on 'Vital Signs'.

Terry recalled, "When we entered Le Studio, I had a really good idea of what we were going for, because they played two tunes live on the road. All four of us had so much knowledge of the tunes." Terry talked about how the band were able to have more impact without compromising their sound. "Even though it's got a lot of in-depth meaning, lyrically it's up to Neil's usual standards. 'Pictures' is presented in such a way that it's immediately accessible to radio . . . or DJs, even though they don't have to get into the lyrics to understand it. It can be enjoyed on a more superficial level, which I think makes a big difference."

Terry was also proud of the rhythmic innovations, especially the fact . . . "that on 'Moving Pictures' we definitely reached a point where the drum sound was by far the best we ever had."

'Moving Pictures' starts in high sonic gear. The sound is crisp as drums and synth slip into a groove on 'Tom Sawyer'. The tune is smooth, with heavy metal spit and spirit thrown in. Neil's drumming is amazing, driving 'Tom Sawyer' onward like a fast current. As Geddy sings of the modern day warrior with 'mean, mean pride', Neil relentlessly propels the song forward. His drum fills are short yet crammed with detail. The song's idealised image of a rock musician

is leavened by the last verse when the warrior exits and 'Today's Tom Sawyer, he gets high on you, the energy you trade, he gets right on to, the friction of the day.'

This seems to be a direct answer to the most hard-driving, negative criticism that was ever written about the band and Neil specifically. Georgia Christgau wrote in a 1977 issue of *Circus* magazine: "Today they promote philosophy too (filled) with self-inflated thought (one) gets from too many nights in front of a throng; 'I'm going to get my money out of you fuckers if it takes two more years'." But beyond any thematic message, the song proved that the band could rock as hard as anyone and incorporate even more complex ideas.

The short phrase during the chorus 'The River' is a great way of tying in the original Tom Sawyer with his modern day counterpart. By the way, the Mini-Moog synth pattern during the middle came from Neil who remembered a part that Geddy used to test his Mini-Moog in soundcheck.

Another footnote. "He knows changes aren't permanent, but change is . . . " is a far cry from "the more things change . . . the more they stay the same."

'Red Barchetta' is inspired by 'A Nice Morning Drive', a short story by Richard Foster dealing with familiar Rush themes . . . the individual against society in a sci-fi setting. But the music and lyrics are much more concise. On an earlier Rush album this could have been a side-long epic. Here it is boiled down to six minutes. Also bringing it down to earth is the car symbol, an archetypical rock and roll icon.

'YYZ' begins with the Morse code signal calling the band home as Neil taps the message out on his crotal. There is so much going on in this song that it takes many listens to hear all of the musical elements employed. Tough guitar leads, funky bass playing and more incredible drum work shoot back and forth. Neil gets his unique sound by smashing a piece of plywood against a chair.

'Limelight' opens with a 'Fly By Night' power riff five years on. This could have been an early Rush metallic tune, but there's a much more accomplished band playing here. Neil is going for the audience's jugular on this one: it's about as frank as you can get. Neil and Geddy have both said that this song is not cruel, but that it is honest. It is both. Self-pity mingles with self-examination of the players, performers, portrayers, and the play itself. The song explains what it must have been like for the band at the hundreds of meetings with people they could not know, who knew all about them. Neil talked about the effects of fame. "You watch somebody play a façade for so long; the façade becomes reality."

'The Camera Eye' focuses on a lighter mood in its attempt to capture what was perhaps the most unique talent of a half-forgotten, early 20th Century American writer. John Dos Passos is not ranked highly in the canon of literature nowadays, but he helped to expand the limits of the novel much like Rush were trying to do with music. And this song, more than any essay about Dos Passos, captures his wide-eyed sense of wonder and ability to see the magic of life. It describes that feeling of place that one can experience in New York or London or any town anywhere that makes each locale unique, and gives it a character and quality of its own.

'Witch Hunt' is part three of what would become the fear trilogy. Parts two and one would come out on subsequent albums. The music paints a cinematic picture while ignorance, prejudice and fear walk hand in hand.

The final song is 'Vital Signs', a tune that introduces a new fascination with the oncoming computer age, not in the abstract, but in the reality that was confronting the band. At the same time the song reprises many of the album's other themes. The inability to absorb all the events flashing by and the struggle to achieve balance. 'Leave out the fiction/ The fact is/ This friction/ Will only be worn by persistence/ Leave out conditions/Courageous convictions/ Will drag the dream into existence.'

With 'Moving Pictures' recorded, the band ran into trouble once again over album design. Hugh's cover concept was his most amusing to date, but it was also expensive, and Mercury would not pay the extra cost. So Rush ended up spending $9,000 of their own money to ensure the cover's quality.

The LP was released in February 1981, and for the first time a Rush recording became a must-play item on album oriented radio stations. It took off immediately, garnering heavy airplay on 98 per cent of the stations.

As these things often turn out, the band's management chose a different breakout song. David Marsden says, "The first time I heard 'Tom Sawyer' . . . I picked it out right away, because that to me is one track that shows their growth pattern more than anything else on 'Moving Pictures'. I think its composition, its writing . . . 'Tom Sawyer' lyrically . . . it's a very contemporary lyric there. There is nothing pretentious about it. You go back to 'Xanadu' and it's a very pretentious thing, but 'Tom Sawyer is not . . . it is good music. It talks about today . . . that to me more than anything else exemplifies the growth pattern of Rush. Interestingly enough, Ray Danniels told me that it wouldn't be a hit. He said "'Limelight' is the hit." They were both hits!

I headed out to Kalamazoo, Michigan, on February 19, to catch Rush as they got their show ready for the 'Moving Pictures' tour. In the months

since I had met them in Philadelphia, I had begun doing interviews for NBC's Source Radio Network. Wing's Stadium was empty except for the band and crew in the early afternoon, and as I walked into the hall I could hear the band playing. I took a seat at the side of the stage and watched them work their way through the new set. Crew members scurried around ironing the bugs out of the new equipment as I saw the trio perform the musical pictures 'Vital Signs' and 'The Camera Eye' for the first time. It was different from a concert performance because the sound engineer was testing the PA system. He might turn down the bass, guitar, drums and synthesizers during 'Tom Sawyer' so all you could hear out in the hall was what sounded like Geddy singing a cappella.

When the sun went down, I got a chance to see the show exactly as the band would play it on tour, a complete concert. The missing element was the audience. Howard manned his battery of lights as Alex, Geddy and Neil blasted through the set. They took a few more chances than they would in front of a live audience as they tried to perfect their approach to the material. After seeing a two-hour-plus perform-ance, I was surprised when they launched into the set once again. This was the last night before the tour began and they worked late into the evening playing the show over and over, trying to get it in the best possible shape for opening night.

During a break in rehearsal, Geddy talked about the factors that were keeping the band together. "We all have a very strong unified cause. We all think alike when it comes to our music, and we all enjoy what we do a lot. We've never had any reason to stop, because our music is still interesting for us to play. There are still a lot of barriers to break through in learning and playing as musicians. They are very tight-knit

personally as friends. When you know what you want to do, it's easier to withstand all the outside pressures. We also try to keep a kind of low-key lifestyle on the road. Because of this, we are not as open to the cracking up that many bands are."

To make life easier for themselves, the band cut down their touring schedule. The Moving Pictures Tour would last six months. While this still far outpaced most bands on the road at the time, it was a considerable relief to Rush. The guys in the band were in their late twenties and it was not possible for them to play three hundred nights a year any more. But since they were playing larger halls they would make more money than ever before.

Geddy also talked about the extra challenges that his ever increasing keyboard work posed when the band tried to translate this to the stage. "It's always a challenge," said Geddy. "The whole idea of being a musician is to keep getting better and to keep putting challenges in front of you so that you improve every aspect of your musicianship. Being a bass player alone is challenge enough, but playing other instruments gives me a better all-around view of what music is. I learn more from having these different points of view. It helps me in writing too, because I start thinking about my music and writing in different ways. As a bass player you are more concerned with rhythm, where with keyboards you concentrate on melody. Playing these two different types of instruments increases my knowledge of music."

The next night Max Webster warmed up the audience in the rowdy college town where Gibson guitars are made. They did a powerful version of 'Battlescar' that went over well with the fired-up audience. This was the kind of crowd that had been listening to Rush for years. The audience knew that Alex, Geddy and Neil could deliver and they were not disappointed. The new material was well received. Older songs benefited from their increased musicianship, but some of the longer epics had to be scaled back in size. Both 'Hemispheres' and '2112' were only performed in part. In a weaker band this would have been a problem. '2112' had really worked for Rush onstage, and it would have been understandable if like The Outlaws with 'Green Grass And High Tides' they had performed it in full for their audience for years on end. But the trio knew they had to progress.

As the tour progressed I managed to catch the band in Louisville, Kentucky, Dayton, Ohio and Binghamton, New York. The more time they spent on the road, the better they sounded. Every date was sold out.

One week I managed to catch Rush two nights at the Capitol Centre outside Washington, DC, Madison Square Garden, Nassau County Coliseum and capped it all off with a show at the Spectrum in Philadelphia.

The Garden show was a particular highlight for the band. They had sold-out the biggest hall in New York City. The only drawback was that the circus was in town and the backstage area smelled of animal droppings!

I began to get to know the band better during this tour. They had heard my work on the radio and apparently liked it, so our relationship was not quite so formal now. Geddy greeted me at the Capitol Centre by saying, "It's Bill Banasiewicz, whose name rhymes with Manashevitz (wine)."

An extra musical highlight of the tour (that would later have several musical consequences) came in early April when the band accepted an invitation to watch the launching of the first space shuttle. The group arrived at Cape Canaveral on a day off. But when the mission was scrubbed because of technical problems, a little bit of tricky scheduling had to be done. The band boarded a plane for a show in Dallas. The launch was rescheduled for April 12, so the band flew back to Florida. This time the launch went off without a hitch. Neil described the lift-off as a once-in-a-lifetime experience. One interesting sidelight: the area where they watched the shuttle take off was called Red Sector A. Once the shuttle was in the sky it was time to head back to Texas for another show.

While the tour was going even better than expected for the band, radio airplay and record sales were even more encouraging. Stations latched onto 'Tom Sawyer', 'Limelight' and then 'Red Barchetta', playing them for months on end. 'Moving Pictures' pushed up to the number three spot on the *Billboard* album charts, remaining there for four weeks. And this was all during a real downturn in the music industry. Established touring bands were cancelling dates and playing smaller halls. Some acts that had achieved gold and platinum records for years were selling less than half their previous totals. Rush became the only band to chalk up three US platinum albums that year. 'Moving Pictures', 'All The World's A Stage' and '2112' all passed the million in sales mark. Rush also received a Grammy nomination for 'YYZ' as best rock instrumental. Individually, Alex, Geddy and Neil found themselves topping just about every readers' poll around as best musicians on their respective instruments, as well as group honours. It was a heady time for the band. The success of 'Permanent Waves' had seemed incredible, and now they were swimming in a much larger ocean.

The one negative event of the period came when

Max Webster broke up. Webster had been gaining popularity in the area that launched Rush, the Midwest, but they were not able to deal with their growing success and they parted ways. Rush had been really pulling for Max Webster and they enjoyed exposing new talent, not to mention the fun of soundcheck jams. The split upset the band and crew. Max Webster were soon replaced as the opening act by another Toronto Band, FM. FM also complemented Rush very well and soon began to make appearances at soundchecks.

I caught the last two dates of the tour at the Alpine Valley Amphitheatre in Wisconsin on the Fourth of July weekend. This concert site was at a resort that was literally in the middle of nowhere. The parking lot outside was filled with Rush fans from Chicago who had driven a hundred miles to see Rush. It was a rowdy few days. Fireworks were shooting off outside the entrance to the outdoor theatre, and hundreds of people were camping outside the parking lot.

But while the audience were ready to celebrate the holiday, the road crew and band were glad that the tour was almost over. Everyone looked tired, and there was much talk of going home and spending time with family and friends.

Geddy looked back at the long road the band had travelled before the soundcheck on July 4. "It was the best tour we have ever done from every aspect," he said. "It was the most successful and we played well on a consistent basis. It doesn't even compare to some of our earlier tours. In a way they were nightmare tours. It's such a whole different world now. In '74 or '75 we were a struggling opening act. You can't even compare that to the tours we are doing

now. I mean the quality of life is so much better. At the same time it's nice that the tour is just about over. At the end of a tour you always have that kind of bittersweet feeling. You are tired and you want to go home, but part of you wants to keep going. That feeling goes away quick, though."

The band had been having success with their soundcheck work as Geddy explained: "As the tour grows the areas we left open to jam on during the show started to get filled in; it became structured. We're just creatures of structure. We always fall into that. We've been starting to have some very interesting soundchecks lately. It's a very satisfying part of the day really, especially when you have been into a tour as long as this one, because the set has become so structured. It's nice when we get together in soundcheck to open up, and loosen up, and experiment in new things. Most of the time you forget what you write there, but when the jams start to get interesting it's a sign that your brain is getting ready to start working on some new material. So I think we will all do some writing at home this summer." Soundman Jon Erickson had been taping the soundchecks so ideas would not be lost.

But first there was the long-delayed live album. The band already had 50 reels of tape from the previous tour and they had recorded more dates on their latest swing through North America. "We plan on mixing the dates from last year's English tour and the material from Toronto, Montreal, Vancouver and Edmonton," Geddy told me. "On this tour we wanted to record shows from the beginning of the tour when we were fresh, and some dates towards the end to see the differences in the confidence of our playing." The Montreal date was shot for a concert film. I urged Geddy to put 'Cygnus X-1' on the upcoming live disc. He said that it was recorded in England, but he didn't know what songs would be used.

Geddy ended the interview by lamenting the fact that part of his holiday would be upset by the baseball strike, since he had looked forward to following the season closely. Ironically his comments would run on the radio the day the strike was settled.

Later that afternoon, during soundcheck, Geddy walked up to his mike and said, "Well, hello! It's good to see you again, and what can we play for you today?" I began to look around to see who Geddy was talking to, but there was nobody else in the amphitheatre. Then suddenly the band wheeled into 'Cygnus X-1'. The air was swallowed by the music's fearsome force. The sound and fury of 'Cygnus' live drowned my heart. The impromptu version ended as the road crew began covering Neil with large curtains

while he was still playing.

The band had the next month and a half off. Then in September, even though all three were supposed to be concentrating on the in-concert record, they found themselves writing new material. It was beginning to look like a repeat of what happened when they decided to shelve a live record the year before. But this time everyone realised that it could not be delayed. There was the matter of the concert film that had been set to be released with the record. Plus the band was itching to make another change in direction, and it would be a good time to release an album that chronicled their development since 'All The World's A Stage'.

While Rush had been frustrated during the mixing of the first live set, they thought it would go differently the second time around. The trio were sure they would be happier with their playing, and to a degree had forgotten how little they had enjoyed the polishing process on the 'Stage' record.

*e*xit . . . Stage Left' was mixed at Le Studio in September. Terry ended up doing most of the work, and for the first time he was to receive the sole production credit. "I guess because I spent so much time in the control room," says Terry, "while everybody else was flying planes, swimming, and driving cars. So that's how it turned out. Normally it's a co-production. The four of us have input into what goes on and how it's done, so it's a genuine co-production. This time around so much of my time was spent in the control room, and of course they had already done what they were going to do. It was already on tape. Basically it was like 'let us know when you finish this tune.' That's really how it went down."

Some tough decisions had to be made. They wanted to get a balance of different types of songs. So some excellent material had to be left out. One of the leftovers, 'Vital Signs', was later released as the B-side of the 'New World Man' single. There was also the compromise between the best technically recorded versions of songs and the ones that had the best feel. For example, Rush were a better band on the Moving Pictures Tour and more advanced sound equipment was used to capture the shows. But during the Glasgow concert on the Waves Tour, the audience spontaneously began singing along to 'Closer To The Heart' and 'The Trees'. It was decided to use 'Closer To The Heart' from that date, but a different version of 'The Trees' made it on to vinyl.

Like the first live record, some overdubs were done, but a mistake or two did slip into the grooves. During 'Tom Sawyer' my favourite drum fill at the end of the song is missing. With all these considerations to take into account, Terry ended up using the English dates on side two and the Canadian concerts on the rest of the record.

The recording is a strong show-case for the band. They are always best on stage, especially when they reinterpret older songs. 'A Passage To Bangkok', 'Beneath, Between And Behind', 'YYZ', 'Closer To The Heart', 'Xanadu' and 'La Villa Strangiato' are better than their studio counterparts. The lone, new

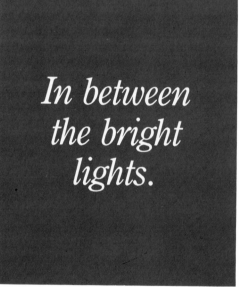

In between the bright lights.

addition is 'Broon's Bane', a classical guitar introduction to 'The Trees' titled after Terry's nickname.

Rush are a different band when compared to the first live album. While they are not as wild, they more than compensate for this with better material and vastly improved playing. The record highlights the remarkable interplay between the members of the trio. The keyboards are an added element on some of the older material, and there is a leap in Geddy's bass playing and vocals. Neil's drumming is an extension of his studio work. The professor always pounds precisely. The jazz-fusion elements Alex had been experimenting with add a whole new dimension to his playing and he really shines throughout the entire record.

As a document of the band, 'Exit . . . Stage Left' differs in two major ways from 'Stage'. Firstly, it is not a record of the band live at one point in their career. It covers two separate tours. Secondly, it covers two different periods in their history as a recording group; the more seventies-style art rock of 'A Farewell To Kings' and 'Hemispheres', and the more stripped down approach of 'Permanent Waves' and 'Moving Pictures'.

Having voluntarily removed themselves from much of the production work on the live record, Alex, Geddy and Neil shortly found themselves bored with their recreational activities. During the long periods when they weren't needed for consultation on different tracks, Alex and Geddy would jam on new material. They were soon working very seriously on individual songs. Neil was putting together lyrics. All three wanted a change. 'Moving Pictures' and now the live record almost seemed to be coming too easily. They needed new challenges. An even further jump into keyboard related material and different musical styles would put up some more walls for Rush to break through.

With a studio so close at hand it was inevitable that some of these new experiments would be recorded. The first one laid down was actually a Jack Secret song that Neil had worked out with Jack and Skip Gildersleeve from the road crew. Eventually Alex and Geddy joined in and 'Tough Break' was recorded. The Jack Secret original has not made it to vinyl, not yet, anyway! The second tune that was completed did. The lyrics were about growing up in the suburbs and 'Subdivisions' was to open a whole new chapter in the band's history. With a heavy synth sound, and 7/8 and 3/4 time signatures, and a new lyrical theme and approach, it was a real departure. While before Neil had written songs for their largely suburban audience, this song was *about* their audience and themselves. This made for a new directness in the band's writing. While before they reflected their audience's dreams, now they were talking about what would happen to much of their audience. And for a great deal of those listeners, the future was not so bright.

Work was also done on 'Digital Man', sections of 'The Analog Kid' and 'Losing It', but with a European tour scheduled for late autumn, there was no time to finish the new experiments.

Hugh came in to work on the cover for the live album. This time he decided to put in elements from every Rush cover to date. Eleven albums was a lot of ground to cover, but as usual, Hugh proved up to the task.

'Exit . . . Stage Left' came out at the end of October 1981. I was very excited about the record, especially since their first live album had been what introduced me to the band. When I discovered they would not be playing in the States until December, I convinced my boss we needed another Rush show. Unfortunately, he would not spring for the whole trip, but he covered part of the expense.

I arrived in London to see the band's multi-night stand at one of the city's largest concert halls, Wembley Arena. All three nights were sold out, quite an achievement when a hometown band like Yes could only fill the place for one night. The show featured 'Subdivisions' and most of the material on the live album. The soundcheck before the second Wembley show revealed the band had made startling changes. Alex and Neil were concentrating on rhythm while Geddy played most of the leads on keyboards. This was a whole new role for Alex, who had always been very much a lead guitar player. It was very interesting to watch them strike out in new directions. After the soundcheck on November 5, Geddy gave the world première of his latest vocal performance on record. 'Take Off' could be heard shaking Wembley.

The comedy single was by Bob and Doug McKenzie of Second City TV. It would make Geddy a pop star of sorts. Bob and Doug were quite a hit on television with their version of Canadian hicks. They decided to record a comedy record, complete with a single that would actually be a song. 'Take Off' ended up taking off in the United States and Canada. On the tune Geddy comes in on the chorus as the special guest star. He sings, 'Take off to the Great White North. Take off. It's a beauty way to go.' Doug explained how Geddy was recruited. "We were friends in school, and we were doing the record, so I called him up. We paid him a few bucks. He came in, put on his toque and sang it."

Geddy commented on the record. "Canada has finally found an identity. I just came in, they paid me my 10 bucks to come in and sing a few words. It was different from any session I've ever done. These two guys were coaching me . . . telling me what to do."

A party after the gig that night showed that Rush could kick out the jams when they wanted. Members of Styx, UFO and Thin Lizzy all kept going until dawn. At the party Neil came up to me and we talked briefly about an interview I was scheduled to do with him the next day. He was trying to be friendly but the whole situation seemed forced.

When we actually sat down to do it, I was nervous. Neil can be intimidating, even when he is not

Geddy with Nancy and son Julian.

trying to be. He has a very concentrated stare and when someone locks eyes with him, Neil is not usually the first one to turn away.

The interview covered a wide range of topics. We started out talking about his influences. "I would say that most of our influences have been European, particularly English. Lately there are a lot of so-called New Romantic bands that I like a lot like Ultravox and Visage. I still like The Police and am also listening to quite a bit of reggae. When it comes to American bands, Talking Heads are an interesting group."

The subject soon moved to the drummer that first inspired him. "When King Crimson first came out . . . Michael Giles was a big influence because he had technical chops that just killed me. I couldn't believe this guy was doing those things. He meant a lot to me because he was the drummer I wanted to be, you know . . . Also the way he played with a total lack of discipline. I love it, just totally show-off, overplaying all over the place, and to this day I think I follow that tendency to a great degree.

"When Bill Bruford left Yes and went out on his own that opened a whole new world of things to me. And then Billy Cobham came along and changed the face of things, and I learnt a great deal from his way of playing jazz."

The topic soon switched to electronic drums. "I'm not into them because I have no affinity for wires, I can't stand electronic things. To me, my relationship with drums is . . . I hit them with a stick and they speak, and it's a very simple relationship, very primal. I also lose patience with them if they don't work. Now, acoustic drums always work. You hit them and they always talk. That's very reassuring to me."

Modern technology brought out Neil's thoughts on the new wave. "Music has gone through the crassness of the new wave, and it's started to come around to a really valid way of looking at things. People like Talking Heads and Peter Gabriel are really going after fresh rhythmic approaches. They are also stripping the music down and getting rid of the unnecessary decoration.

"Now, although we have always been interested in a more stylistic approach to music, and making it better, perhaps, in terms of putting more into a song than it really needs, we've found ourselves changing.

"We've started streamlining a bit. Our songwriting now comes from a stronger rhythmic point of view. We find a pulse that feels really good and build our changes around it. Whereas in the past we tended to do the reverse. We would find a melodic passage that we liked and go nuts on it rhythmically, and put so

many time changes and meter changes in it that it became like an octopus."

The subject turned to the longer concept pieces on the earlier albums. "I think all those numbers came from a lyrical premise, where I was involved with an idea that demanded that kind of musical length. And now my writing is much more concise, and I'm more interested in stating things briefly and clearly, rather than decorating them with all kinds of metaphors. There's also the fact that we've shown off a lot musically and we don't necessarily have as much to prove as we did. On our first few albums we weren't that good, and it was something we were concerned about because we wanted to be good. I think we've reached the point now where we at least feel that we have reached a certain technical level of expertise, and the confidence that comes with that allows us to be less concerned with all of that experimentation and all that frittering around."

Neil talked about his role in the band's song writing. "I'm never just a lyricist. I'm always writing songs for music. So I tend to put into my phrasing certain twists that will demand a certain kind of musical interpretation. I'm always thinking of the musical foundation within the context of the lyrical framework."

With lyrics on his mind Neil started to discuss his literary influences. "I'm basically your self-educated guy. I'm a high school drop-out. I tend to go from writer to writer, but it's almost been an historical progression. When I first started, I got interested in really simple things and went back to mythology, for example, the early Greek and Anglo-Saxon tales. I then worked my way up to the Victorian writers, people like Flaubert, Dickens and Hardy. Now, I find myself reading the North and South American writers of this century. I really like John Steinbeck, F. Scott Fitzgerald, and Gabriel Garcia Marquez. Basically the new world writers of this century represent to me the thrust and energy of the times."

With all these different styles of writing that appealed to Neil, I asked him about different musical genres, and their effect on Rush. He described how the reggae beat was becoming more important to the band. Neil said he understood why rock drummers were attracted to it, its strong emphasis on the upbeat really enchanted western percussionists. And the whole group had absorbed them because, "We've always tried not to be restricted in style, and if for example Alex is interested in classical guitar, or I'm interested in reggae or ska, or Geddy wants to go after a fusion-type sound, we are all willing to explore it.

"Added to this is that personally we've remained really strong friends, and we are able to give each other room. I don't think that's the case with a lot of bands."

The subject went back to drumming. Neil explained why he played with the butt end of his sticks. "When I first started playing and I would break the proper end, I could not afford new sticks. So I would tape them up and turn them around. It's also partly that I like to use a lighter stick, but at the same time I want to hit the drum head with a lot of muscle. So using the butt end is a way to get a lot of surface area struck, without having to shift a couple of pounds of drumsticks around. This is especially important because I like to do a lot of quick little things and really rapid little movements that really aren't possible with big logs.

"At the same time when I'm keeping a beat with a high-hat, a snare, or a bass drum, I like to lay almost

the whole length of the stick across the snare, from the rim right in. I've found, for example, on some of my tom toms, especially the higher pitched tom toms, that I get quite a different sound by laying about five or six inches of wood actually on the drumhead. Then as it depresses it, it stretches down on the head and de-tunes it. So it gives it more throatiness."

I then asked Neil if it was a problem switching back and forth from his regular kit and sticks to other percussion instruments and mallets. "Once I get down a series of moves and counterpoints of balance, shifting from one side of the kit to the other, it's all right. Given the wide lateral spread of my drumkit, I can't sort of sit in the middle and reach everything, so I'm constantly shifting my weight. Where it can get hard is when you are hitting the glockenspiel . . . you have a margin of error of about an inch and a quarter."

He then discussed how he branched out to other percussion instruments. "I guess I got into it because of musical greed . . . just wanting to do more. There were points in songs that I didn't feel right playing drums, but at the same time, I didn't feel right just sitting back there and doing nothing. So it was a way I could complement a musical passage in a more melodic way."

Discussion of technique soon brought Neil back to his starting days as a drummer. "It was never a question of discipline for me, because I loved it so much. I came home from school every day and played for two hours or as long as my mother could stand it. I never had to force it. Discipline is a good thing, but I think when it's an obsession, as much as that it restricts your life, as much as I did miss out in my teenage years, because I spent so much time playing drums, and watching bands and so on . . . I could have spent that time driving around in cars and picking up girls. I might have missed the whole social scene in my teenage years, but it's a trade-off you make and I probably wouldn't have done it out of discipline, because I was a typical teenager. I was lazy and rebellious and not very interested in anything. There is one other thing I should mention. I had a drum teacher who once said to me if I worked hard enough, I would be a drummer one day, and that's all the encouragement I needed. I just tried not to copy one drummer, but 20 drummers, so eventually I developed my own style."

The two-hour interview went much better than I expected. Besides any material I would be able to use for the radio show, I felt I had gained an insight into the passion and intelligence that went into the band's music. You could almost feel it as Neil sat leaning slightly forward with his legs crossed, chain-smoking, as torrents of words flowed from him. It almost seemed like a human encyclopedia was speaking as we jumped from topic to topic.

Before the band left Wembley late that evening, they had Kevin Flewitt line up the fans who had been waiting hours on end to catch a glimpse of Rush. The fans caught more than a glimpse because Alex, Geddy and Neil signed autographs for every last one of them.

A few days later came the best show I have ever seen a band perform. The place was Edinburgh, Scotland; the hall, The Royal Highland Exhibition. Even though it was very cold, there were about 3,000 people outside the venue some five or six hours before the show because the promoter had sold all the tickets on a general admission basis. The interior of the arena was literally a skating rink with no seats at all. And it was almost as cold inside as it was outside.

To make matters worse, the soundcheck was a disaster. Geddy's equipment was not working and he was very angry. The band as a whole were upset because they had needed a police escort to get from the airport which was just a quarter of a mile away from the hall. Another crowd of kids had been waiting for them at the landing strip.

When the doors finally opened, it seemed like a burst of people had been stuffed into a cannon and shot into the hall. Actually it was more like a machine gun because the stream did not stop until it looked like 8,000 had been crammed into a space that could comfortably hold half that amount. A quick look outside showed that there were another 3,000 people trying to get in. They began banging on the doors in unison looking for a way inside. At one point another burst of teenagers managed to crash the gates and dissolve into the crowd.

From the moment the band came onstage, the audience was with them. A sea of arms punted in perfect time with the music. The kids sang along with every song, even the relatively obscure ones like 'By-Tor And The Snowdog'. The audience inspired the trio to deliver a performance way above their usual high standards. Even more than in Allentown, it was one of those magical moments when audience and group are at their very best.

About halfway through the show, the heat of the crowd began to raise the temperature in the hall. People were sweating as if it was the middle of summer. At the exits to the venue, where the cold and the hot air met, giant clouds of fog were created. It cast a strange glow over the entire arena. By the time Rush ended the concert with 'La Villa Strangiato', I thought that much of the audience would not have enough energy to leave. Amazingly, everyone was able to walk away.

When I got back to the US my boss liked the interview with Neil and I was able to convince him that we needed a major two-hour radio special on Rush. A month later I was in Hartford, Connecticut, to interview Geddy and Alex. I talked to Geddy first. He was relaxed. It was hard to believe that he would be playing in front of 20,000 people in just a few hours.

He started off talking about the European tour. He seemed happy with the results although he said many of the halls were larger than he expected them to be. He added that even when they played in more intimate settings, it was different to the small venues they played at the start of their career.

"In the early days," he said, "you are really struggling and those smaller halls, they don't seem

that small to you at all. They are big, important shows. So you are always moving forward and going somewhere and you are pretty hungry. Whereas now there is more of a relaxed feeling about playing smaller halls, once you have played the big places. After one of the (European) shows Neil turned to me and said, 'There are a lot of Rush fans in the United States who would give their left arm to see us in a place like this,' and I think he was right." The band would keep this in mind and eventually do something about it.

We then got on to the subject of the group's insistence on continuing as a trio. "It's a direction we have moved in . . . to be able to approach material that a trio would not normally be able to do. If you bring in enough instruments and make yourself adaptable enough, it's possible. Just the introduction of different sounds at the right time makes it feel like a

whole different thing. It's a breath of fresh air that blows in on the guitar, bass, and drums when suddenly everyone switches to synthesizers."

He then talked about the problems of putting together a live album. "It's a very painful process listening to your own past performances over and over again. It's not like making an album from scratch where you are involved in the creative process. Because with a studio album you do not know where you are going next. It's like you are exploring . . . you are building the album as you go. But a live album is all patchwork. You are trying to pick the best performance . . . and fix mistakes. You are trying to make this instrument sound better or make that vocal have more impact. It's really all repair work."

I then asked Geddy about the growing popularity of Canadian bands in the United States. Many groups had received US record contracts in the wake of Rush's success. Geddy was reluctant to lump all the acts together. "I know a Canadian accent when I hear one, but I don't know that bands from Canada have any unified approach. They are all different."

While we were speaking of the differences I asked him what it was like to hear his own music on the radio. "A musician is forever trying to look at what he does and see what it is, and he can never do that, because it is impossible to be objective. I think in a situation where all of a sudden you hear your music on the radio, you have a tendency to try to zone in and figure out what you did. I mean what does it really sound like? But I really hate hearing myself in public. Like if I walk into a party and somebody puts a Rush record on. I find it very embarrassing."

The conversation ended with a few words about the band's motivation. "We started playing because we thought a musician would be a real cool thing to be. Then as you learned how to play, you wanted to learn how to play better. And as you started writing songs, you wanted to learn how to write better songs . . . it sort of never ends in a way."

A few hours later I sat down for my first interview with Alex. He was the most easy going of the three, as likely to tell a joke as discuss a guitar solo. While he was not as theoretical as the other two about the band's approach, he had a remarkable memory and could often recall the exact date or place where different events in Rush's career had taken place.

Alex was thinking about the differences between touring and his home life. "It's nice to have a family, to have that stability, and it's also nice to experience the craziness of being on the road. They both work well against each other even though they are opposites. You also can't stay home too long. But I must admit as

the years go on, it gets nicer and nicer to stay home."

While talking about home Alex soon began to discuss how it felt to see some of his old friends now that he had 'made it'. "I know for me when I see those guys . . . they find it difficult to relate to me. Although I haven't changed really . . . all the things around me have. Plus it's (music) something I was doing even back then, so it's not an alien weird thing for me. But they look at the success and they relate you to quote 'rock stars' they read about, and it's strange. Of course there are a few friends that never change. They are always a joy to see."

The subject soon drifted back to music. Alex brought up Geddy's voice and the negative reaction it got from radio programmers and rock critics. "Gedd's voice was in a high enough register that it offended a lot of people which never really bothered us. We always thought it was a kind of good thing, because it brought our audience closer to us. We weren't the kind of band that you would hear on the radio . . . so it developed into a cult following. I think because we were not all that popular to the people that did not know the band well, we were all that more important to the ones that did, and we felt it."

And that cult status put the band in the position of not having to worry about hit singles. "We always thought the album was the important piece of work. Once it was out of our hands, if the record company wanted to release a single, it was up to them. We never sat down and wrote a song and said . . . 'This is going to be a hit single.' We always . . . I don't think consciously, maybe subconsciously, steered away

from anything like that. The album was the result of our time in the studio . . . all that sweat . . . it wasn't just for one song."

When it came to the band's future, Alex was optimistic. "I'm really excited about the new material, it's going to be a real departure." The band's early versions of 'Subdivisions' and 'The Analog Kid' pointed to the direction they would take. As it turned out, a direction that Alex would not be happy with.

But first the Exit . . . Stage Left Tour had to come to a close. There was a final pair of dates at the Meadowlands in New Jersey on December 21 and 22 1981, and the second night marked the last time Rush played all 12 minutes and 33 seconds of 'Xanadu'.

Then it was time for the trio to take a two and a half month holiday before they would get back together to continue writing new material. The future looked good. Three songs were already more or less completed and they had an extended period of time to work on the rest of the album.

Rush's record sales continued to escalate. 'Exit . . . Stage Left' was a top ten record and sold more than a million copies. This was impressive considering that double-record live albums had gone out of fashion. As always, their back catalogue continued to move off retailers' shelves. 'Moving Pictures' was approaching the double platinum mark, and 'Take Off' was a top ten single in the States. As 1982 began, Rush found that they were nominated for a quartet of Juno Awards. They were even competing against themselves for Album Of The Year with 'Moving Pictures' and 'Exit . . . Stage Left'.

Right: at the launch of the
space shuttle.

*t*he band spent most of March working on new material. With Terry on hand again, everyone was reaching for a new direction. The band even had one of its few arguments with Terry over 'Digital Man'. He did not like it, they did. Usually they would come around to his point of view. This time they did not.

A short tour was scheduled to tone the band up for its next trip into the recording studio. The gigs were nicknamed by Howard the Tour Of The Nadars (tornados), and Louisiana, Mississippi and Florida were covered. Rush débuted 'The Analog Kid' and 'Subdivisions' with 'Digital Man' and an instrumental version of 'The Weapon' played only in soundchecks. I managed to catch the last three dates. I had just helped produce my first major radio show about the band and they were pleased with the results. While at earlier shows I had felt a bit of an outsider looking in, I now sensed that they considered me a friend. As confirmation I even got a nickname at an all night bowling party in Lakeland, Florida.

Everyone in the group and crew has a monicker, most of the names having been developed during the long hours spent passing time between gigs. For example, Geddy is known as Dirk, Howard is Herns, Liam is LB, Skip is Slider, Tony Geranios is Jack Secret, Alex is Lerxst . . . and Neil is known as Pratt. I was bowling on a team with Alex and Neil. I went off to the bar for a minute and when I returned Neil called me B-Man. I could not understand why, and then I looked up and saw that the lit-up score sheet had the name B-Man, probably because scorekeeper Larry Allen (Shrav) did not have a clue how to spell my last name.

The last date of the tour on April 12 in St Petersburg saw the band retire another old favourite as 'By-Tor And The Snowdog' barked for perhaps the final time onstage.

As Rush headed into the recording studio, they were ready for a radical change. The success of their last three records had seemed to make life a little too safe.

Clearly they had used the extra time the live record had given them to take a shot at remodelling

themselves. The heavy keyboard textures of 'Sub divisions' formed a platform to build upon, while Alex wanted to expand his rhythmic role in the band and Geddy was anxious to use the keyboards as the lead instrument on at least some songs. While this sounded like an interesting idea in theory, it would cause problems and create tensions in practice. The band entered Le Studio on April 21. They would not leave until July 15.

Although work on 'Chemistry' was completed around this time, the band had actually composed it back in 1981 on the 'Moving Pictures' tour during a soundcheck jam. When Alex and Geddy were going through the tapes of the jams, they discovered that one day they had written what became 'Chemistry' and for the first time all three members collaborated on the lyrics of a song.

Another blast from the past would inspire them. The whole band wanted to try to recapture the thrill of watching the space shuttle launch. Using actual audio tapes of the launch sequence, they tried to recreate the final countdown in musical terms.

'Losing It' was designed as the album's studio production number. FM violinist Ben Mink actually gets the lead spot in the song. This uncharacteristic song was the kind of risk taking move the band were looking for. Here was a group that for the most part depended on its abilities as a trio, doing a tune where someone outside Rush was the lead player.

While recording, Rush found they had an extra four minutes to fill up. They had fairly strict ideas about how long a record should be, even down to the length of each side, so they embarked upon what would become known as 'Project 3:57'. If the song passed the four-minute mark, it would have been more difficult to master the recording. Neil spent a few days getting together some lyrics. The music was written in one day and put on tape a day later. This stood in marked contrast to the long and careful trial and error approach of many of the other songs. 'Subdivisions' was eight months old by the time they hit the studio.

Change was the name of the game on the recording of 'Signals', even down to the brand of

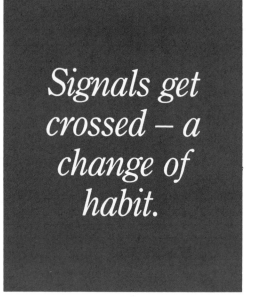

Signals get crossed – a change of habit.

recording tape used. Unfortunately, some of the signals got crossed. While the album contains some great music, it is also the first time in Rush's career that the overall sound quality of a record takes a step backwards. The strain of trying to redirect their sound proves too much. If 'Permanent Waves' and 'Moving Pictures' have sharp production, 'Signals' is a little on the dull side, and the main reason is the diminished role of Alex's guitar playing, which is way back in the mix and has little bite even when he is playing a great solo. To be frank, it just does not sound as if it was recorded quite right. There is a greatly reduced Rush attack on many songs, and even the keyboards, which are supposed to be the highlight of the record, have the same flat quality. And the drum sound, which was really fantastic on 'Moving Pictures' also takes a step back.

When it comes to individual tunes, there are some great ones, even if the sound is not up to Rush's standard. 'Subdivisions' fairly drips with emotion. Its theme of suburban alienation is well sketched and delivered, and Geddy does a great job of switching from a synth lead to a bass line during the chorus, but you can barely hear guitar until the closing section of the song.

'The Analog Kid' brings the guitar up a bit, but nowhere near the level of earlier records. Still there is some meticulous musical interplay between Alex and Geddy. The song expands on the themes and dreams of 'Subdivisions' with its tale of future hopes.

'Chemistry' has the same metabolic mix as 'Vital Signs'. Once again Alex's great guitar work is kept too far down in the mix to hear his fluid phrasing. Neil's cymbals and high-hat sound good but the toms are muffled. The lyrics could get taken as being all about types of human interaction, or it can be seen as applying to very specific individuals. 'One-two-three/add without subtraction/sound on sound/multiplied reaction/H-2-0/No flow without the other/oh but how/do we make contact/with one another.' This little joint venture lyric could have come straight from the latter day works of Samuel Beckett.

'Digital Man' takes up a slightly ska-like beat. The guitar drives the song forward, while Neil locks into the beat and keeps it going. 'Digital Man' details a soul under observation who observes his watchers, but he also seeks escape. The drums are the song's lead instrument, which may explain why this song is one of this drummer's favourite Rush tunes.

'The Weapon' or Part Two of Fear continues Neil's trilogy in descending order. If 'Witchunt' focused on the power and hysteria of the mob, 'The Weapon' deals with the way individuals are kept down. The drum beat is the closest Rush ever came to being a disco band. Of course you have got to realise that when a beat goes through the hands of Neil Peart it will always have a unique stamp . . . something most disco and electro-pop does not.

'Project 3:57' or 'New World Man' continues the band's experiments with exotic rhythms. Even more than on 'The Spirit Of Radio', reggae infiltrates the music. Some of the sonic problems of the other tunes are toned down on 'New World Man'. The song is a little sharper than most of the material.

'Losing It' is a gentle, peaceful song on which Ben Mink plays eloquently a beautiful violin part. The production sound works in this song's favour: Jean-Luc Rush in action. Missing in action is Alex Lifeson.

'Countdown' attempts to bring that long remembered shuttle experience to life. While Geddy was later to say that the song comes across like a textbook, it does have drama, and is not dull. The moment comes alive. Here is a band that has always been fascinated by technology trying to describe a leap forward in man's development.

What must have been most upsetting to the band was that at the same time they were forging forward musically they were taking a step backwards sonically. Geddy had predicted that the record would be a dark album; it was, but not in the way he intended. A troubled period was about to begin for Rush. Yet, at the same time as they were trying to face these troubles, they would have their highest charting single and their most successful tour ever.

Nineteen Eighty Two was a tough year for touring rock bands. Double bills of former stadium headliners became quite common. The summer gigging season saw many groups play 10,000 seat outdoor venues instead of the 20,000 seat hockey arenas they had filled in years past.

In this atmosphere Rush prepared for the New World Tour in Green Bay, Wisconsin, at the very end of August. Band and crew spent a week getting the show into shape. Defying the economics of the day, Rush were expanding their show. Another truck full of gear was added, bringing the total to five tractor trailers, including a larger stage, more lights for Howard to use, and a bigger sound system.

On September 3, the New World Tour began in earnest. Despite the weak concert market, the show was sold-out. 'Subdivisions' was illustrated with shots of high schools and shopping malls. 'Countdown's' drama was multiplied by actual film footage from NASA of the space launch. The crowd went wild not only for the band's music, but also for more than 900 lights Howard had to work with. (Their previous high had been 400). As Herns did his best Jon Lord imitation at the lighting board, the beams of light vectored down upon the stage. The emotion transmitted into the massive lighting rig combined with the music to create an unearthly show. Hern's signals were turning green and red and yellow, not blue, and roving searchlight beams slashed the night.

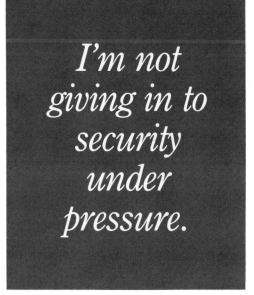

I'm not giving in to security under pressure.

The sound system was upgraded both in size and in the way it was placed. If the production on 'Signals' was inferior, the sound on tour was not. By placing their bass bins on the floor of the arena and not on the sides of the stage, they were able to give the audience an unobstructed view of the show, and also up the bass feel in the hall. The place literally shook when heavy low end vibrations came through the crackling speakers.

After the show Neil talked about some of the changes that were taking place in the band's music and his own approach to lyric writing. Neil said he thought 'Subdivisions' hit on his own experiences of growing up and those of much of Rush's suburban audience. While he talked of feeling outside in the tense times of the 1960's and also the concurrent desire to conform, it was clear that the subject was deeply personal. At the same time he understood that some would find it hard to listen to songs that outlined their and his reality, as opposed to the ideals of, say, '2112'. "Some people would say it's a better trend in my writing, for others it's worse, but for me it is necessary."

He moved on to the band's desire to change. "When we are making a new album we are trying to make it different. We want it to sound different. We want it to affect the listener in a different way. So, therefore, experience doesn't always help you. This album took us much longer than albums in the past. There weren't any technical reasons and there weren't any personal reasons for that, just the simple fact that we wanted something different made it that much more difficult to attain . . . to the point where from day one we set up the equipment in a whole different manner. My drums were on the opposite side of the room from where they had been for the last two albums, because we were determined to get a different sound from the ground up.

"But I think it's also the law of diminishing returns at this point. In the beginning we started off low, so were able to improve at a greater rate. With the last three or four albums I think with all humility, we reached a certain level of confidence in our ability. And consequently the improvements and rates of change have to be in smaller increments. Once you get to a certain level, it's that much harder to extract a lesser degree of improvement. And that's basically the situation that we are in."

A situation that had required the band to spend an entire year preparing 'Signals'.

As the tour progressed, sell-out date followed sell-out date. 'New World Man' broke out on top forty radio stations, leaving Rush with their first hit single. It climbed as high as number 23. A minor hit for a fully-fledged singles band, but amazing for a group

that were almost complete strangers to the format. FM airplay was a foregone conclusion.

The band were glad to be back on the road. After so long in the studio, it was liberating to be doing what they felt they did best . . . playing live.

The new ease came into play at a show in Milwaukee on October 9 where Geddy, during 'The Spirit Of Radio' saluted the Brewers' play-off success with a little rewrite . . . 'One likes to believe in the freedom of baseball.'

A three-night stand in Toronto during November saw the hometown crowd anything but blasé. The shows were all sold-out, and the audience reaction enthusiastic throughout, the complete opposite of their unsuccessful Varsity Stadium gig. But Neil expressed reservations about playing Toronto . . . "I hate playing at home. There is so much tension in the air. People come crawling out of the woodwork for tickets and passes. 'Remember me, I was your paper-boy six years ago'."

Boys Brigade, a new wave dance band, entertained the band and their friends at an after-show party where members of Rush danced along to the latest in techno pop stylings. Geddy talked to Boys Brigade about producing their début album. The

proceeds from the third night's show were donated to UNICEF.

The band spent the rest of November and much of December playing the East Coast. What had once been one of their weakest areas was now one of their strongest. Multiple dates were played in Washington, New York and Philadelphia. The band got into Philly a day before the show, and Geddy, always the sports fanatic, went to check out the Flyers in the Spectrum where Rush would be playing the next night. Between periods the electronic scoreboard flashed RUSH IN CONCERT DECEMBER 13 AND 14 . . .

SOLD OUT. A large segment of the audience cheered, and Geddy, sitting quietly with his hair tucked under a baseball cap, gave a huge smile.

A concert review on a local radio station a day later from Bill Fantini captured the mood of the concerts. 'Another night of Rush and Rory Gallagher at the Spectrum tonight. Last night's performance was one Rush after another . . . computerised lights spotting and flashing . . . some great video on the huge screen behind them . . . including SCTV's Count Floyd vampire to intro the tune . . . 'The Weapon' . . . school halls and shopping malls . . . and backs of cars throughout 'Subdivisions'. Now I thought they were just going to show the Columbia space shuttle shooting into the air during the song 'Countdown', but they had the whole launch sequence. The show opened with 'Spirit Of Radio', 'Tom Sawyer' and 'Free-Will' . . . and I don't know what you were doing from 10:21 to 10:27, but Neil Peart was doing one hell of a drum solo during their encore 'YYZ'. Great show from Rush, another one coming up tonight.'

The band then took more than a month off for the holidays during which Geddy produced the début album for the Boys Brigade. He had high hopes for the band as did Howard and Ray, their managers. But, despite a solid performance and lots of club dates, the band were never able to gain a large following. Still, it reflected Rush's growing interest in outside projects. Geddy was talking about branching out into film work. Alex had a growing obsession with flying and he occasionally said that he might like to try to act. Neil was writing articles for *Modern Drummer* magazine and writing fiction on the side. All three began to talk more frequently about solo projects. While they had mentioned the possibility of such work in the past, now it came up in almost every interview they did. Much of the work on 'Signals' started out as a G. Lee solo project. The band also began to express doubts about 'Signals'. The strain was starting to show.

This was apparent at a show in San Diego in February just after the holiday break where their performance was sloppy and the sound was weak. About the only part of the show that was up to their usual high standard was the lighting. However, the crowd thought they were playing a great show. After the concert the band didn't want to see anyone. So, I went back to talk to them. They asked me what I thought. I said, "Don't ask me because I'll tell you." Neil said, "That bad, huh?" We spent the rest of the night getting drunk, laughing, telling jokes and having a good time. Alex tried to drag me onto the bus which was heading for Tucson, but I couldn't go.

Even though I have seen the band many times, and expect quite a lot out of a performance, there is no one more critical than Alex, Geddy and Neil of their playing. They know when they play badly, and appreciate it when someone is willing to tell them. There is apparently nothing worse than doing a bad show and then having someone tell you that you were great. Of course, a rotten Rush concert is still better than most others.

The band continued to think about the results of 'Signals'. The more time that elapsed, the more dissatisfied they became. While sitting at the crew meal with Geddy and Ben Mink backstage at the Hollywood Sportatorium in March, Terry Brown arrived on the scene. "What are you doing here?" said Terry "He's our tour reporter," replied Geddy. Broon was down to discuss the production of the next record. It was time for a show-down. During the course of several days of meetings, it was decided that Terry would not produce the next album. He had been with the band for a decade, and had been called 'the fourth member of Rush' by the band themselves. They realised that they needed a change, but as Neil later said, it was "like cutting an umbilical cord."

"It is no easy thing to tell someone that, after all this time, you want to work with someone else for a change - and still harder to be told it. It was tough for us and tough for Terry. We have been through so much together and he has contributed so much to our development and refinement - both as people and musicians. It was awkward, difficult and a bit painful, but we had to do it or always wonder, 'what if we had?' While objectively one may recognise the right thing to do, subjectively it's sometimes too easy to rationalise the easy way out. We had to cut the umbilical cord."

Alex later told the *Milwaukee Journal* that . . . "After 'Signals' we were at a point where we wanted to know how someone else would treat our music. We had become so close with Terry that it was difficult to be unsure about anything."

Geddy told *Scene* magazine that . . . "The main problem was that we had tried so many different experiments the last few years that we lost sight of the essential Rush sound. We needed to regain our confidence and our trust . . . "

Whatever the artistic reasons for the change, the personal cost was high. Terry was not just a co-producer, he was a friend, and Alex, Geddy and Neil always believed in sticking behind people loyal to them. Yet, at the same time, they needed to show fidelity to the music that had brought them so far. Terry would later produce the soundtrack for a

concert film of the band's performance, but he was out as their studio producer.

As their US tour came to a close, the band ended up doing a large indoor show in Syracuse, New York, and everyone was a little nervous about playing inside the massive Carrier Dome. This meant that Neil was hitting his drums even harder. The band seemed on edge most of the day. Geddy had been sick from the night before, but the show had to go on. Prior to the concert, everyone stayed out of the dressing room, except me. Neil sat cross-legged, smoking, his head buried in a book. He would occasionally glance up and laugh at Lerxst and Dirk and their ethnic imitations. The pair can be very, very funny.

It was unusual that there was no one in the band's dressing room. Most of the time the crew are in and out all night, just like a giant family. They are each other's best friends; they eat, work and travel together. Unlike certain other bands, there is no separation between Rush and their crew.

I left Alex, Geddy and Neil by saying, "It's going to be a great show; I can feel it." "Fuck off, B-Man!" they shouted back.

Despite their fears, the gig was great. Rush went over very well as more than 30,000 fans rocked out to the beat of their music.

Backstage after the show was a festive scene as the band, crew and friends partied the night away. "You were right, B-Man, it was a great show!" yelled Geddy. "Have a drink," said Neil. It was a day and night difference in attitude before and after this Syracuse show.

Next came another European tour. While in England, the band talked to a series of producers, including Steve Lillywhite, known for the distinctive sound he brought to U2, Big Country, The

Psychedelic Furs and Peter Gabriel. Lillywhite agreed to work with Rush but two weeks before they were supposed to start work he backed out. The only explanation they got from his manager was that "Mr Lillywhite has decided that he is not the right person for the job."

The band were initially taken aback. But they quickly regrouped and made up another list of possible choices. Among those they almost tried was Rupert Hine but he too backed out at the last minute.

At the end of July, Alex and Geddy travelled to New York to play at the 'Celebrity Tennis Jam' with John McEnroe and Vitas Gerulaitis, a rare opportunity to see the pair play on stage with different people.

Alex jammed with blues great Buddy Guy. Gerulaitis and McEnroe also joined in. Buddy Guy tried to cut Alex in a guitar duel but Alex was able to hold his own. Gerulaitis was not a bad guitar player. McEnroe should probably have stuck to tennis.

Next came Clarence Clemmons' band. Three or four songs into the set, Clarence introduced Geddy who strolled onto the stage, Fender bass in hand. He played along with skill and a real feel for his fellow players, and just as with Alex, a whole new side of his talents was displayed. The highlight of the night came on some fantastic bass runs during Otis Redding's 'Sitting On The Dock Of The Bay'. The time he had spent in Ogilvie back in the late 1960's paid off.

In August, realising they at least had to start working on new material, the band began putting together some new songs. Neil's writing had taken on a darker tone, reflecting the band's problems, his own personal state, and some of the issues he was reading about in newspapers. Yet, paradoxically the band were energised by the experience. Since they had to rely on themselves, and they felt kind of rejected, they were able to focus their anger and disappointment into new material. In three weeks, they had rough versions of 'Between The Wheels', 'Kid Gloves' and 'Afterimage'.

But, before they could continue work on the songs, they had to prepare for a series of shows scheduled at New York's Radio City Music Hall from September 18 through 23. Since they had not played together live since the beginning of the summer, they needed a week to rehearse. After all, the shows were at one of Manhattan's most prestigious theatres, and they wanted to put in a strong series of performances. Originally, they thought they would have most of the new album in good shape with a producer at this point, but that wasn't the case. Cancelling the gigs was out of the question, because they were important

for the band, serving as a warm-up for the studio. In the past their pre-recording shake out tours had generally been done in smaller cities. Now they were going to play the biggest city in North America for a solid week in an intimate hall. The time frame was different because they weren't actually ready to start recording.

At a rehearsal the night before the first show, as I watched them run through their set, I roamed around the music hall checking out how they sounded in every corner. "How does it sound up there B-Man?" Geddy yelled to me through the PA. I held my thumb up in the air as I leant over the very top balcony. The band then ripped into the 'those who wish to B-Man' version of 'Limelight'. Also played that evening were the 'plumbers who fix your sinks' version of 'Temples Of Syrinx' and the 'Mr Herns loves to Babylon' version of 'Digital Man', as well as the new material. 'Red Sector A', 'Kid Gloves' and 'The Body Electric' were played for the first time. They featured these songs in the set throughout the week's performances.

Neil looked like a kid in a candy store while checking out the music hall after rehearsal. He roamed through every corner of the grand building. All five shows were sold-out. Rush fans came from all over the country and Canada to see them in such a setting. A host of other rock bands came to check out Rush! Bono and Adam Clayton of U2, members of Blue Oyster Cult, Utopia and Foghat.

At the shows themselves, the band improvised through many of the instrumental passages of the new songs, and thrived on the atmosphere of a smaller hall. To a Rush fan, it was the ultimate treat. The encore was 'YYZ'. It featured Neil soloing on his brand new red Tama set, and the first appearance of his electronic Simmons drum kit. He had finally joined the electronic drum revolution, even though he had said a few years before that he had "no affinity for electronic drums and wires." Neil, realising that "constant change was here to stay," decided to move forward rather than be left behind.

Towards the end of the stand Alex invited me to visit the band at Le Studio during the recording of the new album. The band were very happy with the shows. They felt they had played well, and it helped to give them confidence to head back and deal with their production problems.

With the Radio City gigs out of the way, the band headed back to Canada to continue the great producer hunt. Rough versions of 'Distant Early Warning' and 'The Enemy Within' were laid down and work was started on 'Red Lenses'. Different people were brought in to listen to the songs and make suggestions about how the arrangements could be improved. Prospective producers were then asked to work with the band for a day or so, to see if they were compatible. At first they were still unsuccessful; they even nicknamed a toy doll 'Roger Kneebend' and called him their producer as a joke.

But then, Alex, Geddy and Neil met Peter Henderson who had worked on several Supertramp records and had extensive engineering experience. He clicked with the trio personally and was eager to do the job. As Neil later wrote, "We were still pretty insecure from our previous disappointments. Would he feel he was the right man for the job? Would he have some complex little problems which he had to sort out? Would he disappear and never be heard from again? Probably! We were determined to ask him first thing in the morning (the band had been having a late meeting) if he would like to commit himself to the project. After breakfast, we told him that we felt he was the man for the job and asked him if he was interested. 'Well' he replied with a dry English smile, 'I wouldn't have come all the way over here if I wasn't interested, would I?' 'All right. Let's go' we chorused."

But the elation did not last long. A new producer with different techniques meant more time recording the album. Added to this were the strains of the past year, and Neil's realisation as he read newspapers that 1984 would be much like an English author had predicted it would be back in 1948.

According to Neil, the down times usually came when one or more of the crew was in a 'black ass' state of mind. "You're working away at a song that you know can be good but it just won't be. You sit in the studio with aching hands and heavy heart, unable to deliver the performance that the song demands, after grinding it out for too long. You listen to a playback of something, and when it's over, no one says anything. Pregnant silences. Avoiding eyes. (Anyone know a good joke?)

"A certain tension descends at these times. The room is silent. Everyone knows something is wrong, but no one really wants to be the one to say 'It ain't right'. To criticise is to presuppose an alternative; to suggest an idea is to put your own pride on the line; to expose your vulnerability to possible rejection and disagreement. To listen to someone else's idea, with which you perhaps do not agree, is a challenge to your objectivity and self-control. It's hard to say what's right about it before you say what's wrong with it. Handle with kid gloves, handle with kid gloves indeed."

By the time I got up to Le Studio, the basic tracks, bass, drums and a guitar part had been recorded. On top of this the band had added some synthesizer bits. Alex was beginning to put down his guitar overdubs, everything from rhythm lines to solos, and he did much of the work over a three-day period, working non-stop for 16 hours at a stretch.

Watching Alex and Geddy work together, it was apparent that they were lifelong friends. Theirs was an easygoing relationship which included a never-ending stream of jokes designed to smooth over the tension and tedium of getting each and every note right. Peter Henderson fitted into this team well; he seemed at ease joking with the pair as the guitar work continued.

Neil was in Toronto working on the cover with Hugh Syme. Once Alex was finished with his main parts, he took a more passive role, watching and listening, and occasionally giving suggestions. Peter and Geddy made many of the actual production decisions. It was clear that Peter was sharing production duties, not dominating them, but Geddy really took charge in many ways, consistently making tough choices that were needed to complete the record. If Neil supplied the lyrics and themes, Alex the rock and roll spirit, Geddy was in charge of making sure it was all captured on tape. Peter supplied the technical expertise and an outside voice.

Lifeson and Lee
(Dimo Safari).

Geddy later told *Scene* magazine that . . . "Henderson was very helpful, a very hard worker. His input made it possible for us to feel that we were taking control for the very first time, like all the decisions were ours. The bottom line was that 'Grace Under Pressure' was more of a Rush produced album because the responsibility weighed on our shoulders."

Neil returned to work on the recording of the lyrics with Geddy, but first Geddy had to add some bass and synth parts. Nothing brought home to me the hard work involved in modern day recording more than watching Geddy lay down his vocal tracks. Alex relaxed, glad that he had done the bulk of his guitar parts; Neil discussed phrasing, his lyrical intentions, and made slight changes if Geddy found a word or line awkward to sing. Peter worked on capturing Geddy's voice. And Gedd was on the spot. He would sing

With Yousuf Karsh, 1984.

single lines over and over again. The lyric 'The world weighs on my shoulders, but what am I to do' must have been done 50 times. Work on the vocal track of 'Distant Early Warning' took 10 hours. Geddy was pretty much all business, and the jokes of earlier days were non-existent. Recording and mixing continued, for three more months after I left, and the band spent a total of five months recording the album. excluding three months spent writing the material.

The title 'Grace Under Pressure' described the way the band saw the whole period. The inner sleeve picture of an egg placed tightly in a c-clamp probably sums up the period best. The band decided to go for a group picture on the back cover, the first with the three posing together since '2112'. Neil said he wanted a Karsh-like photo, referring to the famed portrait photographer Yousuf Karsh. So they asked him and he accepted. It was the first rock band he had photographed and Geddy said he thought Karsh was disappointed that they were not wearing leather and acting like 'rock stars'.

Neil later wrote: "It was an inspiring and elevating experience to sit before the lens of the portrayer of kings, queens, presidents, popes, astronauts, authors, scientists, and film stars. And there he was taking an album cover photo for bums like us! It was wonderful to see, at his 75 years of age, his tremendous energy, creativity and swift changes of mood. He provided us with a memorable and broadly applicable quote when told that the lights in the room were not independently adjustable: 'That is not an answer that I can accept'."

The final album marks not so much a step forward for the band, as a return to form. Alex's guitar reappears with a fury that Geddy later considered an over-reaction to the synthesizer textures of 'Signals'.

'Grace Under Pressure' is a dark album, and it took a heavy toll on the band. When I first heard the record at Florida's Spring Training in March, Geddy turned to me and said, "You don't think the band could go on forever, do you?" I replied, "Maybe not forever, but at least for another 10 years." What I later learned was that Gedd was trying to tell me that the band were thinking about breaking up. Although they would later discuss this more fully, at first they kept pretty much to themselves. The individual songs reflect the darkness of the time. One of the strongest is 'Distant Early Warning'.

'Afterimage' is written about a close friend of the band's who died in a car accident. It's a very personal song, but although it has a tone of sadness, it tries to capture the beautiful memories that Neil had of Robbie Whelan who was killed in an auto accident near Le Studio and to whom the album is dedicated. The sense of a friend trying to explain how much someone who is not there and never will be again, meant to him, is captured in the call and response between Geddy's vocals and Alex's guitar on the chorus.

'Red Sector A' is a hopeful song amid darkness. A man is in a futuristic death camp, his fate unknown. For his father and brother it's too late but he still must help his mother stand up straight. Geddy sings as if he understands at least partly what such an experience would be like. His voice carries the tone of hope through the fear and horror. Even though the outcome is unknown, a vivid picture comes to mind of the man carrying his mother to freedom. Neil's drum fills are a metaphor for the smoking guns. Musically it is a quintessential latter-day Rush song, complete with complexity, dexterity, sharpness and provocative passion.

'The Enemy Within', the final but actually the first part of the Fear Trilogy, completes a song cycle begun with 'Witchunt'. In this section, the fear is that which is inside us, and not externally created. A great chorus . . . 'I'm not giving in to security under pressure/I'm not missing out/On the promise of adventure/I'm not giving up/On implausible dreams/Experience to extremes/Experience to extremes.'

Neil plays a drum part on the song that reminds listeners how dexterous he really is. At one point during the chorus Neil plays the high-hat with his left foot, then kicks his foot over to the closest bass drum, throws in an accent, then it's back to the high-hat. On the very next measure he hits another accent on a claptrap in an odd time. His left foot moves back and forth between three percussive instruments, while his right foot plays the other double bass, his right hand rides the bell of a cymbal, and his left hand plays the snare, with drum fills thrown in to top it all off.

'The Body Electric' is the album's futuristic sci-fi number. When Neil handed Alex and Geddy the lyrics, they asked if it was inspired by the film 'Blade Runner'. Neil replied that he had not yet seen it. There is also a Twilight Zone episode bearing the same name.

'Kid Gloves' contains what is perhaps Alex's best recorded guitar solo, a welcome change of pace on an otherwise dark album.

'Red Lenses' sounds like a cross between Jimi Hendrix, U2 and Peter Gabriel. The song is constructed around a complex drum pattern during the chorus. Neil wanted to base the piece on that rhythm. Lyrically the tune highlights what has been a slow

change in Neil's approach to words. He began reading 20th century poets like T.S. Eliot, along with prose writers of that same period. On songs like 'Red Lenses' Neil tries to play with clichés and subvert while giving them new meaning at the same time. And the words give pleasure on two levels, first by their very sounds and then by their meaning.

'Between The Wheels' is about pressure, and returns to the gloom of much of the rest of the album. Alex's guitar really jumps out. A lyric from the song puts across some of what they all must have felt at the time. 'We can go from boom to bust . . . from dreams to a bowl of dust.' Before the album was released, the band made videos for 'Distant Early Warning', 'Afterimage', 'Body Electric' and 'The Enemy Within'.

'Grace Under Pressure' was released on April 12, 1984, and by the beginning of May, Rush were rehearsing for the Grace Under Pressure Tour in Albuquerque, New Mexico. The rehearsals went smoothly, and Alex, Geddy and Neil sounded better than they had during the warm-ups for the Signals Tour, perhaps because they had spent even longer working on the material.

On May 7 it was dress rehearsal night. "I want you to go out there and be a tough critic, B-Man," said Neil. Lee Tenner from the crew and myself were the only ones in the hall and after every song we would yell, clap, stamp our feet and hold up Bic lighters. The band had passed the test; Rush were ready for their very critical audience. Rush fans follow every note, solo, drum fill, rhythm, and vocal very, very closely. A Rush concert puts Alex, Geddy and Neil under the microscopic eye of their loyal hard-core fans. This makes Rush even more critical of their performance. They want the show to be perfect.

The tour opened the following night and a highlight of the show was the first in-concert performance of the Fear Trilogy. While it had been recorded in descending order, it was played live in ascending order. The performance piece was interesting in part because 'Witchunt' had been designed as a studio production, and the band had never intended to play it live, but advances in synthesizer technology now made it possible. The band members had to go back to the recording and figure out how to play 'Witchunt'.

A day later, I conducted the strangest interview I've ever done. Alex rented a Cessna single engine prop plane to show me his flying skills. I took along a tape recorder and tried not to get airsick as we swooped over the desert. It was 'Fly By Day' for real. Here's a brief excerpt:

"I've always thought there was something beautiful about airplanes, just the fact that a large piece of

not just playing the shows; they were headlining above Gary Moore (their opening act for most of the tour), .38 Special, Bryan Adams and Ozzy Osbourne. With these 60,000 seat shows the group had reached the pinnacle as far as live performance was concerned. But the gigs convinced them that this was one mountain they wanted to climb back down. At the Houston Astrodome, Neil looked out at the mass of people on the playing field and said, "Look at all these people; we're a hockey team, not a football team. We're a hockey team."

While the band fared OK with such large crowds, there was a tremendous soundcheck in Dallas. Neil was pissed off because Geddy came back late from an extra inning baseball game, and while Neil may never admit it, he always plays best when he is angry. He is the kind of person who if he says he will meet you at 11.00 sharp, he will be there at 11.00 sharp. Adding to the atmosphere was the fact that the Cotton Bowl was pitch black except for a few white lights on the stage at midnight. This jam should have been filmed!

July 8 saw the band play the Pittsburgh Civic Arena. Nearly 10 years before on August 14 Neil had played his very first gig with Rush at this arena, opening in front of 11,600 people. This time they were headlining and the place was SRO with more than 16,000 people crammed inside. At the show Neil and I reminisced about the show a decade ago. He said that I was the only one to acknowledge his anniversary of sorts. I had bought each band member a bottle of their favourite booze, and a card telling them what their music had meant to me.

In many ways it was a different band that played in Pittsburgh that night. They were now first-rate musicians and could headline in front of crowds of more than 60,000 people. At the same time a variety of pressures seemed to be pulling them apart. Yet they were playing better than ever on this tour. The more hard rock oriented sounds of 'Grace Under Pressure' gave the band a kick in the butt on stage.

In other ways they were more mature. All were now married, with children, and maintaining a relationship while travelling and recording for six months or more at a time was difficult. Spending time cultivating these relationships now seemed more important. It was around this time that the band realised there could very well be an end to Rush; not that they wanted to break up or anything, just that one day the band would no longer be around. The press got hold of this and completely blew it out of proportion.

On tour Rush and their crew were hardly choir-boys. As well as the lasers he used with the band

machinery can fly in the air is really an incredible thing. So that of course sparks your interest, and also the challenge of getting a pilot's licence while being on the road. It's very difficult to find the time to be able to do it. This is what's known as a stall." The next sound was my gasp as the plane plummeted towards the ground. After several landings and take offs, we eventually landed on earth. Alex had logged his 171st hour of flight.

Neil was becoming a cycling maniac. He began to cycle between gigs if they were close enough. After one show he took his bike off the bus in San Diego, and caught up with the band 150 miles and one day later in Los Angeles.

In June the band played a pair of huge festivals in Texas. Every year there are two 'Texas Jams' held at football stadiums in Dallas and Houston. Rush were

Howard had purchased a small model for himself. One night he was demonstrating how it worked by shining it from his hotel room window into an apartment building across the street. The beam was so strong that it went through the windows of the adjacent apartments.

He was actually able to interrupt a family's late night meal by shining the light right on to their supper table. One woman began running around her apartment as Howard tracked her with the beam. This went on for over an hour before his phone rang. It was hotel security who told him the police were on their way. Minutes later, there were knocks on the door. When the cops asked Howard how his laser beam found its way into half a dozen apartments, he said he was trying to repair it and had not realised that it was shooting across the street. After a 20-minute interrogation, the police accepted his explanation with the provision that no more repair work be done that night. It turned out that many of the people thought that the light was some sort of guidance system for a sniper's rifle!

On Bastille Day in Montreal, July 14, Alex tried to resurrect their song of the French Revolution in the tuning room before the show, but it had been so long since he had played it that he had difficulty remembering it.

Rush continued touring throughout the summer. They had slowed down quite a bit from the old days of 13 nights of shows and then one rest day. Now they played no more than four or five shows a week, and would take seven days off for every three weeks on the road.

On September 20 and 21 the band played two hometown days, and to add to the pressure the band decided to film the concerts. One full Rush show had been filmed a few years before 'Exit . . . Stage Left', but this time Alex, Geddy and Neil decided to go all out. Additional lighting and stage production would be used. Noted film director David Mallet, who worked with the band on their 'Distant Early Warning' video, was in charge of the visual end of the shoot. And appropriate to a hometown show, Terry Brown made a return appearance. The result, while probably the best visual rendering of the band onstage to date, still does not totally capture the way they are in concert. You simply have to be there.

The day before two sold-out Spectrum shows in November, Neil and I rode our bikes to the Valley Forge and back. The next days we pedalled through South Philly right into the Spectrum dressing room.

"Hello, Philly!" Lee lashed out. "It's good to be back in the home of cheesesteaks and the B-Man!"

I was freaked! My favourite band were sending me regards in front of 18,000 Philadelphia fans. The reason I'm bringing this up is because I think it's a very important point as to the kind of people Rush are. If a friend of theirs is having personal problems, troubles etc, Alex, Geddy, Neil and even the crew will bend over backwards to help them through the period, cheer them up, encourage them, give them inspiration. This is a major factor contributing to the longevity of the band and crew. If someone in the Rush family falls from grace, others will be there to lift them up. They are truly a family.

Later that night there was a wild, raging, all-night party on board a tall ship docked on the Delaware River.

Four concerts in Japan and two in Hawaii would close the P/G world tour. Days were set aside for sightseeing different territories throughout Japan, Hong Kong, Hawaii and even the People's Republic of China.

First came the Japanese dates. Considering Rush had never played the country, they had a substantial following there. They have a Japanese fan club, and their records are released by Sony Records. The first two shows were played in small 3,000 seat theatres in Nagoya and Fukuoka.

seemed like a regular Rush concert. But there was one distinctly Japanese element: a man who operated what was in essence a traffic light for the audience. Green meant the crowd could clap as they wanted. If it looked like people were starting to get out of hand, the yellow light would be changed to red. This meant the concert was cancelled. The man in charge of the light was given authority to make this decision. The traffic system had been installed after several people had died at a concert that had got completely out of control. Rush managed to get the yellow light on a few times during the course of the concert. It was Herns who controlled the red lights.

Alex later commented on Japan: "It was interesting. I really enjoyed it, but I didn't come away from it feeling like I had really done something that I'd been waiting for all my life kind of thing. I think going to Texas for the first time was more of a highlight than going to Japan. I always wanted to go there, and the people were very friendly and polite. I wasn't as overwhelmed by it as I thought I'd be. Playing in Japan was OK. If I'd had my own equipment, it would have been better." Alex used Music Man amps for the tour.

From Tokyo we moved on to Hong Kong. One day was spent exploring the city before the much anticipated one-day trip into the People's Republic of China. A hovercraft took us to the mainland via Maccau. Then everyone boarded a bus for China. The difference between Hong Kong and the People's Republic of China was incredible. The Communist nation was much poorer. There were beggars everywhere on the other side of the border. The tour included a stop at a village where merchants would try and sell you anything 'five Hong Kong dollar'. They would yell in Chinese-style English while holding up the item in question. Chinese accentuated English is more tonal than the Japanese version, and sounds better.

Soon it was time for the long flight to Hawaii, and suddenly we were in a society that seemed familiar. And finally the tour came to a close at the NBC Arena with two dates in Honolulu. There was a larger proportion of women than usual at a Rush concert, and the most intense scent of sensimilla I've ever smelled. Only in Hawaii!

On the way to the last show, Alex announced to everyone in the limo, "I want to quit the band . . . I'm gonna leave." I saw the band from the third row at that gig . . . I was convinced that it could very well be the last time they ever played together. I didn't know it at the time, but, according to Neil, "Alex says that at *least* once a week."

The band found the politeness of the audience strange. There was no applause between the songs and the crowd made very little noise even after their most fiery instrumental breaks. At first the trio thought they were bombing in a major way, but when the show ended everyone stood up and cheered. They apparently did not want to interrupt the show (too polite!). These concerts were performed with rented amps and staging. Tama drums made Neil a copy of his set just for the tour.

The final Japanese date was in Tokyo at Japan's most famed concert hall, the Budokan where we experienced another side of Japan. There were 16,000 people, including a few Americans from the military posts in Japan. Still, the audience was 70 per cent Japanese, and they went crazy, singing along with the band and clapping between every song. It

Some time off lowered the tension level considerably. If as Geddy said, "Rush were now an album by album proposition," the realisation that this was the case liberated the band. The future commitments bearing down on the band were no longer much of a burden. And looking back on the most recent tour showed that as a playing unit the band had never sounded better.

Added to this was that the more time Rush spent at home, the more they realised that they were not yet ready to retire. Inactivity became boring after a while. On February 10 Geddy sang with the Canadian Artists Against Hunger in Toronto. The name given to all the famous Canadian musicians was Northern Lights.

So, after a few months at home, they began thinking about a new album and some more challenges for themselves. Alex, Geddy and Neil had seen studio production become even more complicated, and they wanted to work with someone who was totally hooked into all the latest developments. They would go for the outside input of someone with wildly different views of how things should be done. Musically they wanted to move towards more melodic songs since they felt that in going for a more rhythmic approach they had strayed from melody. Neil was going for more lyrical complexity. He wanted to be able to have his writing appreciated on several levels. In the material that was taking shape in his notebooks were specific references to things he had done and seen, topics as profound as atomic bombs and the barriers that divide nations.

With a whole new batch of ambitions the band were ready to start looking for a new producer, and Gary Moore hooked them up with Peter Collins. Collins was known primarily as a high-tech singles producer, and while this may have seemed like an odd choice for Rush, they wanted somebody who would bring a radically different perspective to the band. Since Collins was based in England, they also decided for the first time since 'Hemispheres' to record the bulk of the album in Great Britain after the initial writing and arranging work had been accomplished.

The band assembled at an Ontario farmhouse in late February. For three weeks they fitted together all the ideas they had worked on during their vacation. They completed work on four songs. A fifth, 'Manhattan Project', was almost complete but Neil was eager to explore different lyrics. All concerned were encouraged by the results. They were ready to go with 'Mystic Rhythms', 'Marathon', 'The Big Money' and 'Middletown Dreams'.

Next came a series of dates that were scheduled in Florida to coincide with baseball's spring training. Four concerts were booked: two in Lakeland and one apiece in Fort Myers and Hollywood. This was heaven for Geddy: while they tested their new material, he could check out exhibition baseball

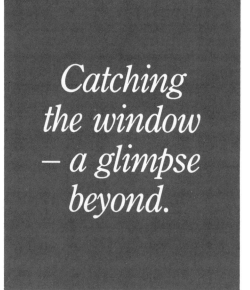

Catching the window – a glimpse beyond.

games. Several players, like his friends Bryn Smith and Bill Gullickson, came out to see a show. A tour rehearsal in Lakeland on March 10 saw the band flexing their muscles. They were a little stiff, but during the four dates the band played loosely. They were clearly trying to get their musical chops back in form for the new album. The tour saw the concert débuts of 'Middletown Dreams', and 'The Big Money'. 'Marathon' and 'Mystic Rhythms' were only played during soundchecks and without vocals.

A few days later relaxing by the pool in Fort Myers, Neil was playing air drums as he listened to a Jeff Berlin demo tape. He had been asked to play on the Jazz Fusion artists' first solo album. The session date was scheduled for right after the tour. Alex also had an outside session lined up. He was to play on a record for the Canadian band Platinum Blonde.

Peter Collins' engineer Jim Barton came down to catch the band in concert. He wanted to check out how Rush sounded live before they went into the studio. Jimbo assured Neil that he could make the drum sound "a hundred per cent bettah!"

Once the outside projects and tour were out of the way, the band settled back in for another intense writing session. They decided to try to write a ballad, 'Emotion Detector'. Neil also finished work on the lyrics to 'Manhattan Project' and 'Territories'.

After the writing was completed, Rush headed for the Manor Studios in England, the 1,000 year old Virgin-owned complex that is mentioned in the Domesday Book. Peter Collins' approach was to prove both unsettling and invigorating for the band.

Geddy told *Guitar Player* magazine about some of the differences: "We recorded the bed tracks in a different manner than we ever have before. In the past, we had been pretty insistent on playing as a trio and trying to get a performance. Even if we ended up redoing the bass or guitar, we tried to get something that felt like a band performance. By doing that, you're sort of at the mercy of circumstance - you're looking for that magical take . . . so invariably you end up doing a lot more takes than you need. And you try to pick the best moments from each one. You start the sessions with high hopes, and at the end, you have a lot of tape, trying to pick those magical moments.

"So Peter Collins said, 'Look, I don't work that way. Let's use a different way and see if it suits you.' He suggested that we use one piece of tape. On that we laid down a click track."

The track was set up so that the band could then add onto it. It served as a foundation that everything else would be placed on top of. They would not have to piece the foundation and frame of the song together at the same time.

"Step two is putting down a rough arrangement using some very simple sounds such as a guitar or keyboard, that basically maps out the entire structure of the song in real time. At that point we still don't have any drums, bass, or anything like that. I put down a guide vocal in the spots where there's supposed to be vocals, and then guide keyboards to fill the sound . . . so we end up with a lot of care taken in a very good guide instrument track. Then, once we have all the drum sounds we want, all three of us start playing on the guide tracks. And after a few run throughs, when we are at a stage where we want to do a take, Peter is not concerned with the bass or guitar; he's just listening to Neil, making sure there is a good drum performance.

"They record the first couple of run throughs, and we get a good live feel on the drum tracks, plus we have all the other main parts in rough form. So, in effect, Neil's playing to a full track. He responded really well to that kind of recording, and I think he did three or four tracks on the record in one take. That method seems to make you focus; you say, this is going to be the take. So, I won't have to look for that mysterious piece of tape."

This method worked well and all the basic tracks were done within a couple of weeks. The band were very happy with Peter's approach. He reminded Neil of the American film actor Edward G. Robinson. "They have a similarity of stature and air of authority." Peter became known as Mr Big to the band. He even smoked cigars.

The next step proved an even more radical change for the band. Andy Richards was brought in to play on the record and to do programming work. While guest musicians had contributed on several tracks in the past, Richards actually became part of the production team, and along with Jim Burgess he came up with new sounds for the band to use. Richards, who was involved with most of the songs on the album, brought extensive experience to the project. He had been a member of the art rock band, The Strawbs, and had also been responsible for Frankie Goes To Hollywood's unique keyboard sound.

Neil later wrote of the experience, "We enjoyed the chance to sit back and suggest things for someone else to do for a change."

But as time went on, Alex got a little bored and picked up a new hobby. Since he still wanted to be at

the studio, he began oil painting.

The electronic experiments were not limited to keyboards. Neil and his drum technician Larry Allen went to a whole batch of music stores in London and rented as many African and Indian percussion instruments as possible. They then spent a day messing around with the drums and sampled the sounds of the ones they liked the most. The sounds were transferred to Neil's Simmons drum set, thereby using advanced technology to capture ancient and even primitive musical instruments. Appropriately these sounds were used on 'Mystic Rhythms'. For 'Territories' Neil made his début as a bongo drummer.

One lesson the band had learned from their difficulties over the last two records was that albums took longer to record. So to break up the monotony of staying in one place, they moved to Air Studios' Montserrat in the Caribbean. They had always dreamed about recording at the studio having previously made albums together in the Great White North and England, not exactly hot spots. While Geddy and Neil were able to take advantage of the sun, Alex ended up spending most of his time laying down guitar overdubs. As evidence of the fun that was had by all, the band's office later received an $300 bar tab run up during the visit.

It was back to England for three months for vocals and additional guitar work. Ironically, the studio, Sarm in London, had no windows. In August, the band moved to Abbey Road Studios to add embellishments like the 30 piece orchestra on 'Manhattan Project', 'Marathon' and 'Middletown Dreams'. The band could not stop laughing as they watched classical musicians playing their material, and the same was true at Angel Studios where a 25 voice choir sang the close to 'Marathon'.

Neil later wrote, "Mr Big wanted us to pull out all the stops on this album, really make it something different, and special." The final mixing work was then done.

Geddy headed to New York City to master the album with Bob Ludwig, and then returned back home to begin work on videos with Alex and Neil.

Hugh, as always, had been in contact with Neil about the album cover. They decided to go with another painting. It features a confused looking boy in a dingy room, holding a remote control to three television sets that he has his back to. In front of the boy is an open window, but he is looking not out of the window or at the sets, instead he is staring at the person holding the cover. The three sets represent Alex, Geddy and Neil, the boy has a power window to Rush. But is the boy closing the window to reality and

just living in Rush world?

"It is pretty abstract," said Geddy on Rockline, "I love the scene of this sort of Billy Bibbot-like character confused as to his reality. The windows that he's looking out are in a sense very powerful windows. This is an album of power. We are talking about different types of power and the way they affect us, and the way they affect him. The boy is a little shaken as to which way he should look and which window is his reality."

'Power Windows' is Rush's most accomplished album to date. The band were able to go beyond their past triumphs and achieve a staggering advance in every aspect of their performance: playing, writing and in the sound clarity of the recording.

'The Big Money' is a parable of how power tries to corrupt. While the song keeps hammering home the theme of monetary success, it also deals with other sorts of power, in venomous asides, whether fame or religion. "It's a Cinderella Story . . . a war in paradise." Sonically, it shows how the band are advancing to a new musical age. The influences of the past few years have been absorbed beyond the point of recognition.

'Grand Designs' to me is about this book. 'Curves and lines - of grand designs . . . ' can be taken as the book itself, or it could be the talk of coming out with a grand design. The music is expansive, echoing the grandeur of unrealised dreams.

'Manhattan Project' deals with the development of the atomic bomb. But its essential message that once the cat is let out of the bag it can't be placed back in, can apply to any major development, whether it be the invention of gunpowder or a big personal decision. It also marks a return to a more cinematic style. And, of course, there is the aural pleasure of an orchestra playing Rush.

'Marathon' is about the endurance one needs to realise those dreams and ambitions that have already been discussed on the first two songs. The sense of the lyrics being addressed at one person comes through very strongly on the chorus. 'From first to last/the peak is never past/something always fires the light/that gets in your eyes/one moment's high/and glory rolls on by/like a streak of lightning/that flashes and fades in the summer sky.' The message concludes: 'You can do a lot in a lifetime/if you don't burn out too fast/you can make the most of the distance/ first you need endurance/first you've got to last . . . ' Again the song does not end. The result is in question. The music keeps pace. An inspirational chorus provides the band with harmonic support as it races through towards the final line.

'Territories' echoes both the band's visit to the Far East, and the divisions between different cultures and people. Specific references to the trip in lines such as 'better people, better food and better beer' which are similar to comments during the early part of the Japan visit can also be seen as the comments of all cultural and military invaders. Neil then compares that pride with the pride of someone who will not be committed to a single territory. The song is a showcase for Geddy's new bass, a Wal, and he gets an amazing tone out of it.

'Middletown Dreams' returns to the subject of dreams. It compares how they inspire some to strive harder to finish the race and others to imagine they can, an impulse that can lead to success or in the case of the middle-aged man to a bottle. Neil argues that this is a very positive song. "The middle-aged man sticks to his dreams," says Neil, "and they eventually become reality."

'Emotion Detector' can be seen as the shattering of illusions and dreams. 'Sometimes our big splashes are just ripples in the pool/feelings running high.'

'Mystic Rhythms' which closes 'Power Windows' is a very different song for the band. Instead of

describing what should be done, it tries to capture things we feel but can't describe. Musically it goes after that sense of wonder which occurs when that feeling of something far beyond us grips our imagination. Neil beats his electronic primitive drum kit on the choruses to capture an exotic sound, using African rhythms, while the keyboards play an Oriental pattern. It is hard to pin down all the musical styles and elements that are being employed.

The whole record fits together like a puzzle that can be assembled in many different ways. Pieces can be put together and the songs have a dream-like relationship between each other. The lyrics on the album are filled with Neil's observations of people's actions, hopes, dreams and failures. At the time, Neil discussed things that motivate him to write a song: "Scraps of overheard conversations provide some material, but it's outrage that really gets my juices flowing. When I see things that are wrong around me, that's when I do a lot of the writing."

Peter Collins really came through for the band on the studio end, giving them sound that delivered on many of their possibilities. By encouraging them to push for the full emotional content of the songs without worrying about how they would play them onstage, he enabled Alex, Geddy and Neil to capture the band's power in performance. The record has the power of a live show without the errors that invariably follow. 'Power Windows' is a flawless record.

But performing this material live would require another change in the band's set-up. Many of the sounds needed had to be stored on floppy discs. It was not just a case of the usual massive preparation the band had gone through in the past; now they would be dealing with a whole new generation of electronic technology onstage. "The technology in music has advanced so rapidly," says Gedd. "There is a synthesizer called an Emulator II which enables me

to sample any sounds, and store them on computer disc. So for the tour we got a whole bunch of these synths and sampled the choir sound for 'Marathon' and the strings during 'Manhattan Project' and other unplayable parts. Jack Secret changes the discs backstage, but physically Alex and I must trigger them onstage."

By the third date of the tour in New Haven, Connecticut, on December 7, 1985, the band had still not got the show into order, and it was obvious. Geddy's vocals were a little rough, and the lighting spot cues were off. The sound was not up to the band's high standard. You could see that they were struggling to play the very complex material. Some of the stored keyboard parts were not loaded in time, so they were not available for Alex and Geddy to trigger. 'Grand Designs' in particular suffered from a noticeable lack of grandeur.

Cliff Burnstein was at the show and in his customary style he made no bones about what he thought. In the dressing room after the concert, he went for the jugular, asking them how long they had rehearsed. At the soundcheck in Hartford the next day, the actual process of setting up the gear and making sure it sounded right took much longer than during tours past. Geddy also insisted that Jon the soundman record that night's show so that he could hear how they were coming along.

The concert was a vast improvement over the night before. The problems were starting to fade. While there were still a few mishaps, they were much tighter, but the band were still unhappy with the show.

By the end of January, when the band hit the West coast, they had mastered the new technology. At the Oakland Coliseum on January 31 everything was right from lights to performance, to sound, to the crowd. Older numbers from '2112' shone along with brand new songs like 'The Big Money' and 'Marathon'. 'Mystic Rhythms' was one of the highlights with inventive use of lasers as Howard made broad brush strokes with the beams on the dry ice released into the air. The most amazing thing about this gig was the fact that Neil had the flu. There was not a person in the audience who could tell. He played great, but was exhausted after the show.

At a concert in San Diego on February 3 the 'Mystic Rhythms' were erratic. In the middle of 'Marathon' the sound system went totally dead, but the lights remained on. Geddy just stood there shrugging his shoulders. After a few minutes the power came back on and Geddy said, "Wow, that was weird." Then they did the entire song over again.

About 20 minutes later it happened again. This time the audience started to boo. When the PA system came back up, the band dived back into the set. After the show I came backstage and, with a grave look on my face, apologised to the band, "I'm sorry guys, I didn't mean to do it, but I was walking around while you guys were playing and I dropped my baseball and I ran after it and tripped over this huge wire and pulled it out of the socket." As the room filled with laughter, I added, "and the worst part was it happened again." It later turned out that there was a bad circuit in the hall which could not take all the power needed to open Rush's live window.

Before the second show in Los Angeles, Neil was very nervous about the clinic which was to be given on the band's stage. Fifty students from the Percussion Institute of Technology would witness the professor's very first drum clinic. Neil shouldn't have been nervous. For 90 minutes he had the students in the palm of his hand. He was informative, funny and interesting. He would explain different drum beats from their original conception to how they've evolved over time, to how the students could do it, to an actual demonstration of the pattern in question. 'The Weapon', 'Tom Sawyer' and 'The Enemy Within' were used as examples. When he did particularly difficult parts all the students would start clapping and more than one blush of red crossed Neil's face. He also showed how important Larry was when it came to performing. While Neil plays Larry has to physically change the settings on the Simmons, and mix Neil's sound and be prepared for any mishap.

By the end of March the band were satisfied enough with their live sound that they recorded shows at the Meadowlands in New Jersey, Springfield, Nassau Coliseum and Philadelphia's Spectrum for use on a possible future live album. The two sold-out shows at the Spectrum were a tour highlight for the band, and may show up in part on a live album in the future. On May 26, the band closed its Power Windows Tour with a two-night stand at the Pacific Amphitheatre in Costa Mesa, California. Band and crew were in a festive mood. At the soundcheck before the final show, Alex, Geddy and Neil broke into an instrumental version of 'Lakeside Park'. I had been after them all week to play that song on May 24 in Sacramento.

At the show that night Neil indulged in some humour that nobody noticed. During the drum solo he did a bit from the Flintstones theme song. He couldn't believe that nobody had noticed it. So, with some assistance from Barney, Fred and Bam Bam, their thirteenth tour of North America was ended.

With the Power Windows Tour closed, it was time for the band to be reacquainted with their families. Geddy's wife, Nancy, flew out to California so they could enjoy a West Coast holiday. Nancy is a successful fashion designer and maintains a hectic schedule herself so these weeks together were much needed for the Lees. Alex flew back to Ontario where his wife, Charlene, and sons, Justin and Adrian, were constructing their new home (Lerxsts's Graceland North). Neil was looking forward to spending the summer with his wife and their daughter. He then took a biking trip through, up, and over Switzerland, planned with his brother Dan.

Neil also took time to record a solo song for *Modern Drummer* magazine titled 'Pieces of Eight'. "In one of the upcoming issues of *Modern Drummer*," wrote Neil, "I have one of those soundsheet deals featuring a piece I wrote and played with marimba and all kinds of sampled percussion stuff, with the acoustic drums over that. I've always wanted to create an all-percussion piece, and this is the perfect tool for that.

Anything can happen – into the present and future.

"*Modern Drummer*'s going to be full of me for the next little while. I have an article coming up about Larry, an article about my new drumkit, the results of the drum test I did in Fort Wayne, and all about my new electronic scene, the soundsheet, and then an article announcing the next big drum giveaway.

"I'm giving away the two old sets of Slingerlands and the red Tamas by way of a contest, in which people send me a taped two minute performance, to be judged by the editorial staff of *Modern Drummer*. Then they will send the 30 or so finalists on to me for final judgement. Should be a lot easier than the 4625 essays I had to read *last* time!" (This is Neil's second drum giveaway).

After a few months holiday, the band began to think about writing. Soundcheck jams were reviewed and notebooks studied. Rush had done their homework. The studio writing sessions started September 27, 1986 at Elora Sound in Ontario, with Peter Collins

again in attendance. "Peter had more influence," says Geddy, "during the writing stage of the new album. He pushed us to improve and try different approaches. The results of his pushing are very different versions of 'Mission' and 'Open Secrets'!"

By mid-December the band had written nine songs: 'Time Stand Still', 'Open Secrets', 'Second Nature', 'Prime Mover', 'Lock And Key', 'Mission', 'Turn The Page', 'Tai-Shan', and 'High Water', but Peter Collins wanted another. "He thought it was important to do one more song," said Geddy, "so 'Force 10' was written the last day of pre-production on December 14." Neil took some lyrics that Pye Dubois had mailed to him and added some verses to them. With the changes completed, Neil handed Alex and Geddy the lyrics to 'Force 10' and they both liked them immediately. A few hours later Rush had written their tenth song for the new album. 'Force 10' is the first time since 'Tom Sawyer' that someone outside of Rush has collaborated on a song. With 10 new songs ready to go, Rush enjoyed the Christmas holiday with their families.

On January 5 the band began recording at the Manor Studios in the UK. "We got the basic tracks done really quickly," says Neil, "all the drums, bass, and basic keyboards were done, along with guide guitar and vocals. We worked with Andy Richards again and he has done some exciting work on each of the new songs."

During the end of the last tour Neil tested different makes of drums at the Percussion Centre in Fort Wayne, Indiana, and hosted another drum clinic. He chose Ludwig, "The new Ludwigs," said Neil, "sound really great on the new album, as I hoped they would, and the new electronic sampling set-up I've been using has given me a much richer choice of sounds for the Simmons kit . . . all kinds of ethnic drums and weird sounds to play with. I also got one of those MIDI marimbas, basically a MIDI controller, with a percussion keyboard that you can play with mallets. I even have a marimba solo on the album (!) which I played on that one."

The drums and bass were recorded with an analogue tape then transferred over to digital tape, in

essence making the record a full digital recording. "It took some time," said Geddy, "to get used to recording with digital tape. It is however very convenient. You can bounce things from track to track without losing a generation. It opens up a lot of areas. You can keep higher quality control. Analogue tape has noise that comes with it, but digital tape is clean."

On February 2, Rush entered Ridge Farm Studios in the UK and an excerpt from one of Neil's letters sums up their stay.

'As to the album, there are going to be 10 new tracks on this one, but don't worry, they're not short or anything. We simply decided that since more and more people are buying cassettes and CDs, why should we be limited by the archaic time considerations of records? So we're probably going to have over 50 minutes of music on this album, which will give a cutting engineer headaches, but means much more scope for us, and of course 'good value for money' (in the English phrase) for the buyer.

'The extra 10 minutes really makes a lot of difference in our conception of the album, as it gives that much more room to explore the strange corners of the things we like to do. Thus there is yet a greater variety of music on this one, and I think it will cover a lot more areas dynamically, texturally, and stylistically.

'The title is going to be 'Hold Your Fire', as the album revolves around the theme of instincts and primal responses to life, as well as the inner drives that, well, drive *us. (All* privileged *information, you understand!) Hugh and I have been working on some cover ideas lately, and we're planning some very different ideas for that as well. (Too early to offer any hints.)*

'But it's all very exciting, and it's all moving ahead, even a little ahead of schedule (shouldn't say that really; bad luck), so everybody is feeling very positive and doing good work.

'At the end of this week we're off to Montserrat, which will be really wonderful. Here at Ridge Farm, an Elizabethan kind of half-timbered place, south of London in Surrey, Jimbo has been transferring things over to the digital machine for the last few days, so our presence hasn't been necessary. So Dirk and I decided to go up to London yesterday, and we had a really wonderful time.

'We each took off for the afternoon, went our separate ways, and had separate plans for the evening, but we got together for a drink in between (at the Savoy Hotel American Bar, don't you know). We were both so energised by the environment, and stimulated by the contrast to being in the studio out in the country, that we just started talking together like new friends!

'The amazing thing was that after all these years of living and working together, we still had a very stimulating and satisfying conversation, each with our separate fields of interest and ambition to feed the conversation. Away from the work environment we just became two friends leading individual lives, which of course gives us things to talk about when we're together.

'I don't know if that all makes sense, but it was just a really nice time, the sort of interlude that's all too rare with people who work together on a day-to-day basis, especially when we are so often obliged to talk about serious questions, and try to make mutually-agreeable decisions.'

On March 1 the band began overdubs at Montserrat, Leeward Islands, West Indies. Three weeks later Rush flew home to Ontario to begin work

at McLear Place where overdubs were finished and embellishments added. Aimee Mann from 'Til Tuesday' was in Toronto to sing back-up vocals on 'Time Stand Still' and 'Open Secrets!' "We had some high parts," said Geddy, "and I sang them, but my voice didn't *suit* the parts, so we thought it would be great to have a female voice on those two songs. We phoned up Aimee Mann and she agreed."

Next came the orchestra recording on 'High Water', 'Mission' and 'Second Nature'. The main arranger, Steve Margoshes, was up from New York. "This guy has written some really bizarre arrangements for our tunes," said Geddy. As Steve departed for New York City Alex said, "We are going to play a couple of days at Madison Square Garden in December. You should stop by, Steve."

On April 24 it was funny to be sitting behind Alex, Geddy and Neil in the control room with a gospel choir singing to Rush in the studio. While Geddy was heard singing, 'Anything can happen/The point of surrender/Anything can happen', the choir sang a crescendo background vocal that built to an exciting climax.

After the recording was completed I got to spend some time with the band, researching all of their personal Rush archives. Geddy has the original stage left television from 'Power Windows' in his living room, while Neil's home features Hugh Syme's stunning original paintings from 'Grace Under Pressure' and 'Power Windows'. Before Neil could say, "What's different about the 'Power Windows' painting, B-Man?," I was saying, "The boy's not looking back through the TV." Neil smiled.

While driving to a Blue Jays game, Gedd played me a rough tape of 'Hold Your Fire'. There were torrents of sound rushing forth from the speakers, from marimba and Wal bass solo on 'Mission' to the orchestral background of 'High Water'. The Ontario evening was a little cold for baseball, so after we saw Kirby Puckett bat, we decided to leave. I really wanted to get back into the car to hear 'Hold Your Fire'.

The record opens with 'Force 10', the final song written in one day. "The fact that it is the opening song shows how strongly we feel about it. We just brainstormed the song in one day," says Alex.

'Time Stand Still' is a very personal song," says Alex, "about experience slipping away. One day you realise that suddenly time has passed. Some experiences in life are gone and it's hard to recapture those feelings."

"'Turn The Page' is the first song we recorded guitars on at Elora Sound, but we then re-did them in England," says Alex. "I used Signature guitars on this album. They are made in Vancouver and sound excellent. I think the guitar stands out more on 'Hold Your Fire'. It's more up front with the keyboards more in the background. We recorded the guitars with two Marshall stacks and two Dean Markely amps. The heads were in the control room with the speakers in the studio. We had a clean, jangley sort of sound that we called Lerxst Sound, and found ourselves going back to use it a lot on this record."

'Tai-Shan' is a personal song about Neil's climb up the sacred Chinese mountain. Legend has it that if you raise your hands to heaven on the mountain top,

you will live for 100 years. 'High Water' is a song which expresses Neil's belief that we come from water, the source.

With the album recorded, final mixing began on May 7 at Studio William Tell in Paris. In June Gedd discussed the new record. "An important growth for us has been a writing outgrowth taken to the production of a song," he said. "In the old days, having to perform material live dictated the production of the songs. Now we don't worry until after the album is completed, and as a result, it's opened us up creatively production wise. Peter Collins has given us appreciation for how much further you can take a song without live performance. He's taught us not to under-produce, so we can do a song justice. It's the method we've developed and it gives us a far more open minded approach as to the recording of a song."

I asked Geddy to compare the album to 'Power Windows'. "'Hold Your Fire' has more melody and more variety," Geddy said. "The variety goes for more extremes. Some songs are direct rock 'n' roll and others have soft, moody orchestral arrangements. Overall, there are more extremes on 'Hold Your Fire'.

B-Man: "Where do you see Rush going in the future?" Geddy: "To the South of France!" (Laugh).

"Making this record," said Alex, "was like being in a car accident except much more fun!" (Laugh).

Towards the end of mixing, Alex flew back to Lerxst's Graceland North while Neil and Geddy had their wives meet them in France. Neil cycled from Barcelona to Paris with his brother Dan.

In mid-July Geddy mastered the album with Bob Ludwig at Masterdisk in New York City. During the summer Rush shot the 'Hold Your Fire' videos and Geddy, Alex and Neil began going through the mountains of live tapes the band have compiled for their next live album. 'Hold Your Fire' was released worldwide in early September.

In the early autumn it was time for the band to start worrying about reproducing the 'Fire' onstage. All the latest technology would be brought in, so extra time was needed to master these complex machines. With the sluggish start they had opening the Power Windows Tour, Rush made sure they were prepared for the Hold Your Fire 87-88 World Tour, set to begin in the Canadian Maritime Provinces of Newfoundland and Nova Scotia where fans have been petitioning Rush to play for years.

The tour was rescheduled in the north-eastern United States and Canada. December will see Rush perform multiple nights at New York's Madison Square Garden and the Philadelphia Spectrum.

The urban development that you see inside the cover is actually a set that is only 18-inches tall. "The set," says Hugh Syme, "was built by Scott Alexander. The road cases are only two inches square. When I look at this neighbourhood, one has to wonder, 'Where is this?' I couldn't resist putting the 'Signals' dog, Spot, next to the fire hydrant. The boy from 'Power Windows' makes another appearance, this time looking out the window, down the street, at something we're not yet made aware of."

"All will be revealed on the forthcoming live LP," says Hugh. "Anything can happen."

RUSH DISCOGRAPHY (UK)

SINGLES

Closer To The Heart/Bastille Day/The Temples of Syrinx
Mercury RUSH 7. January 1978. (12″ version also includes Anthem).

The Spirit of Radio/The Trees
Mercury RADIO 7. February 1980. (12″ version also includes Working Man.)

Vital Signs/In The Mood
Mercury VITAL 7. March 1981. (12″ version also includes A Passage To Bangkok and Circumstances).

Tom Sawyer (live)/A Passage To Bangkok (live)
Mercury EXIT 7. October 1981 (12″ version also includes Red Barchetta (live)).

Closer To The Heart (live)/The Trees (live)
Mercury RUSH 1. December 1981.

New World Man/Vital Signs (live)
Mercury RUSH 8. August 1982. (12″ version includes Free Will).

Subdivisions/Red Barchetta
Mercury RUSH 9. October 1982. (12″ version also includes Jacob's Ladder; also available as 7″ picture disc).

Countdown/New World Man
Mercury RUSH 10. April 1983. (12″ also includes The Spirit Of Radio and excerpts from a Rush interview; also available as 7″ shaped picture disc).

The Body Electric/The Analog Kid
Vertigo RUSH 11. May 1984. (12″ version also includes Distant Early Warning; also available as 10″ red vinyl disc).

The Big Money/Territories
Vertigo RUSH 12. October 1985. (12″ version also includes Red Sector 'A' (live); 7″ gatefold sleeve version has Middletown Dreams as 'B' side; 7″ doubleback also includes Closer To The Heart and The Spirit Of Radio).

Time Stand Still/Force Ten
Vertigo RUSH 13. October 1987. (12″ version also includes The Enemy Within (live) & Witch Hunt (live); (12″ picture disc also includes The Enemy Within (live)).

Notes 1. In the USA and Canada Rush's singles' discography differs considerably to the UK. Their first single, in 1973, coupled Not Fade Away with You Can't Fight It on Moon Records, two tracks which have yet to be issued in the UK.

ALBUMS

RUSH
Finding My Way, Need Some Love, Take A Friend, Here Again; What You're Doing, In The Mood, Before And After, Working Man.
Mercury 9100 011.

FLY BY NIGHT
Anthem, Best I Can, Beneath Between & Behind, By-Tor And The Snow Dog; Fly By Night, Making Memories, Rivendell, In The End.
Mercury 9100 013.

CARESS OF STEEL
Bastille Day, I Think I'm Going Bald, Lakeside Park, The Necromancer: (i) Into Darkness, (ii) Under The Shadow, (iii) Return Of The Prince; The Fountain Of Lamneth: (i) In The Valley, (ii) Didacts And Narpets, (iii) No One At The Bridge, (iv) Panacea, (v) Bacchus Plateau, (vi) The Fountain.
Mercury 9100 018.

2112
2112 – Overture, Temples Of Syrinx, Discovery, Presentation, Oracle: The Dream, Soliloquy, Grand
Finale; A Passage To Bangkok, The Twilight Zone, Lessons, Tears, Something For Nothing.
Mercury 9100 039.

ALL THE WORLD'S A STAGE
Bastille Day, Anthem, Fly By Night, In The Mood, Something For Nothing; Lakeside Park,
2112 – Overture, The Temple of Syrinx, Presentation, Soliloquy, Grand Finale; By-Tor And The Snow Dog,
In The End; Working Man, Finding My Way, What You're Doing.
Mercury 6672 015.

A FAREWELL TO KINGS
A Farewell To Kings, Xanadu; Closer To The Heart, Cinderella Man, Madrigal, Cygnus X – 1.
Mercury 9100 042.

HEMISPHERES
Hemispheres – (i) Prelude, (ii) Apollo, (iii) Dionysus, (iv) Armageddon, (v) Cygnus, (vi) The Sphere;
Circumstances, The Trees, La Villa Strangiato.
Mercury 9100 059.

PERMANENT WAVES
The Spirit Of Radio, Freewill, Jacob's Ladder; Entre Nous, Different Strings, Natural Science: i) Tide Pools
ii) Hyperspace iii) Permanent Waves.
Mercury 9100 071.

MOVING PICTURES
Tom Sawyer, Red Barchetta, YYZ, Limelight, The Camera Eye, Witch Hunt (Part III of Fear), Vital Signs.
Mercury 6337 160.

EXIT STAGE LEFT
The Spirit Of Radio, Red Barchetta, YYZ; A Passage To Bangkok, Closer To The Heart, Beneath Between &
Behind, Jacob's Ladder; Broon's Bane, The Trees, Xanadu; Freewill, Tom Sawyer, La Villa Strangiato.
Mercury 6619 053.

SIGNALS
Subdivisions, The Analog Kid, Chemistry, Digital Man; The Weapon, New World Man, Losing It,
Countdown.
Mercury 6337 243.

GRACE UNDER PRESSURE
Distant Early Warning, Afterimage, Red Sector 'A', The Enemy Within; The Body Electric, Kid Gloves,
Red Lenses, Between The Wheels.
Mercury VERH 12.

POWER WINDOWS
The Big Money, Grand Designs, Manhattan Project, Marathon; Territories, Middletown Dreams,
Emotion Detector, Mystic Rhythms.
Vertigo VERH 31.

HOLD YOUR FIRE
Force Ten, Time Stand Still, Open Secrets, Second Nature, Prime Mover; Lock And Key, Mission,
Turn The Page, Tai Shan, High Water.
Vertigo VERH 49.

4/92 (13519)